YOUR
DAMN
MANIFESTO

DISCOVER THE KEYS TO PERSONAL TRANSFORMATION AND BRINGING YOUR BIGGEST DREAMS TO LIFE

BEVIN FARRAND

Book Cover by Theresa Goodrich

ISBN: 979-8-9888625-1-2

For Guinevere, Johnathan, and Mirastela
You are my sun, my moon, and all my stars

For Mark
My love, you are in my heart, forever and always

Do Your Own DAMN Thing!

♡ Bavin

CONTENTS

Introduction	1
Take the DAMN Trip	4
Movement Over Mindset	14
The PAD Method™	20
Uncovering Your YES	27
Remembering How to Dream	29
Focusing in	33
Gut Check	43
Red Light: The TRIP Filter	63
The Parking Lot Method	77
Cultivating Inspiration	83
Your Six-Dimensional Why™	93
Crafting Your DAMN Manifesto	118
The Power of Your DAMN Manifesto	129

What Next: Bringing Your DAMN Mani-   136
festo to the World

Your DAMN Manifesto Resources   139

Finding Your DAMN People   141

Acknowledgments   151

About the Author   154

INTRODUCTION

I never intended to create a movement.

Steve Jobs was right when he said, "You can't connect the dots looking forward; you can only connect them looking backwards." I didn't set out one day to create the Take the DAMN Chance movement. It was only after a series of Deeply Challenging Experiences that I started to think about how I navigated through the world. It was looking backwards that showed me how I had gotten through. But once I saw it, I couldn't unsee it.

I wasn't born knowing the Do the DAMN Thing Method®. Which is great news for you. Because every single thing I'm going to share in this book is *learnable.*

Too often we confuse talent with skill. People are born with talent and, yes, it does help. But all *skills* are

1

learnable. What I'm going to share in this book—about bringing your dreams to life—is all based on skills you can learn. You can take what's in this book and use it to bring any dream to life.

Any. Single. Dream.

It doesn't matter if your dream is to start a business, or write a book, or star in a movie, or expand your family, or have a deeply connected and passionate relationship, or....

Will some of your dreams take longer to bring to life than others? Of course they will. But the key to bringing *any* of your dreams to life is to craft a powerful DAMN Manifesto. That is the critical piece that is so often missing in dreams, and why people give up on them.

But that is no longer the case for you.

Do you want to live a life filled with regret at the dreams you *didn't go after?* Or do you want to live a vibrant life, full of incredible things that *you* have made reality, that makes people stop and go, "Damn..." If this is your one big, bold, wonderful life—how do you want to live it?

By the end of this book, you will have your own personal DAMN Manifesto and be well on your way to bringing your big, bold dreams to life.

Before you start I want to tell you one thing that I believe with all of my heart: what you want in life *matters.* Your dreams *matter.* You *matter.*

Now get ready to Do the DAMN Thing.

With so much love,
Bevin

TAKE THE DAMN TRIP

O n Mother's Day of 2019, my husband Mark gave me four bottles of Bordeaux wine and a card written in French. This was a little confusing since Mark didn't speak French—but I did. I quickly realized that he had booked us two tickets to France for my 40th birthday, which would be in November. Thirty-nine hours on the ground, just the two of us.

Probably seems a little strange that he gave me this six months in advance (not as romantic sounding as sweeping me out the door, right?) But we had two kiddos under two so there was a lot of planning that needed to be done; Mark and I loved to plan. He was an engineer and I was a project manager. Let's just say there were a lot of spreadsheets in our house.

We quickly set to work deciding who would be staying with our kids. I calculated how much breast milk

I would need to pump for our then-four-month-old. We requested the time off work.

Things seemed to be falling into place for us. We had our two beautiful children, both born via IVF after a long fertility journey. We had built our Dream Home along the river in a small town in Ohio. We were both excelling in careers that we loved.

Two weeks later I was ready for my annual review and was expecting a promotion. I'd been with this company, in a role that I loved, for nearly two years. I logged on to my Zoom meeting; but, instead of getting a promotion, I got let go.

We were reeling. We were very much a two income family; in fact, I was ⅗ of that income. We had just taken money out of our savings so I could take a full three month maternity leave after giving birth to our son, Johnathan. We'd bought a van for our growing family. We had thought things were going so well. We never expected this.

Of course, one of our immediate thoughts was, "We should definitely cancel our trip to France. It's completely irresponsible and, frankly *crazy*, to go on a trip to France when one of us is unemployed." But Mark had bought travel insurance so we could literally cancel up until the day before our trip. We decided to give ourselves time to figure things out, to see if I could find a new job.

A few weeks later we were out walking with our kids on the country roads when I told Mark that I didn't want to look for a job. I could feel the little engineer gears in his head grinding to a stop.

"What do you mean you don't want to get a job?" he asked. "We need the money."

"I know," I said. "But this is not the first time that I've lost my job. This is the *third time* in under ten years that I've lost my job, for one reason or another. And I'm tired of it. I don't want to put the financial health of our family into the hands of any *one* person, ever again. I want to start my own business—doing what I've been doing for the past 10 years for smaller companies and entrepreneurs."

As I said before, we loved a good spreadsheet. I made one to show Mark that even if I didn't make another penny going forward, we would run out of money on October 12th. Maybe that sounds really scary to you but, to me, it was so comforting. Because I knew that the likelihood of me *not making another penny* was slim to none. I wasn't going to just sit down on the side of the road and wish and hope. I was going to get clear on my goals and get into action.

Mark and I agreed to give it a try. If I could make $5000 by the end of August then it was a valid concept and I'd keep going. In the meantime, I'd still send out resumes and look for a job, just in case.

When June ended and I hadn't made a single dollar, I was a little nervous but no less committed. And when I made my first $1000 in July I was excited...but still nervous. But by the end of August I had made the agreed upon $5000 and my business was picking up momentum. By the time we were ready to leave for France I had made $35,000 and Collaborate.Work, my business, was growing.

And yet we still thought that maybe we should cancel our trip. Yes, my business was growing, but it hadn't yet stood the test of time. Maybe we should reschedule after we were more secure.

But we didn't cancel. We flew to Bordeaux, spending as much time in airplanes as we would on the ground. We wandered through the city, going from wine bar to cathedral to brew pub to monument to bakery to cathedral to wine bar...you get the idea. It rained the entire time but we didn't care. I got to spend my 40th birthday with the love of my life, in a beautiful city neither of us had ever visited before, just the two of us. We reconnected to who we were before we got married, before our stressful careers took off, before we had kids.

Mark even looked at me at one point and said, "I feel like I'm rediscovering the real you."

We flew home from France, feeling refreshed and reconnected, just in time for Thanksgiving week. Thanksgiving has always been my favorite holiday and this year would be a big one. We had 25 people coming—my family, Mark's parents, our best friends. Mark had taken the whole week off to get things ready around the house. We took our 2-year-old daughter, Guinevere, to her first movie theater show and spent time as the Farrand Family of Four that we had built and loved.

Thanksgiving was chaotic but wonderful. We spent the day with our best friends and family, watching Guinevere dance around and Johnathan crawl after her.

The next morning I had scheduled a massage, a birthday gift to myself, and Mark and the kids were going to spend the morning with his parents. I let Mark sleep in.

When I went to wake him up, he wasn't breathing. He was ice cold.

And I started screaming. I was screaming for him to wake up, screaming for his mom to call 911, screaming for the paramedics to hurry.

And in the middle of all my screaming I looked up and saw my two-year-old daughter with her hands pressed so tightly over her ears, trying to block out the noise and so I whispered, "Please wake up. I can't do this without you."

But none of it mattered. Mark passed away in the middle of the night from undiagnosed heart disease masked by systemic lupus. We had no idea this was coming.

All of a sudden I was the solo parent of two kiddos under three, the sole financial provider with a brand new business that had not yet truly been tested, and I was doing all of it without my best friend and the love my life and, honestly, my biggest cheerleader by my side.

It felt impossible. It felt like my life had been ripped apart, dumped out, twisted around, and then tried to put back together but the pieces didn't fit. There are days and weeks that I barely remember. My family and our friends stepped in to keep me going, bring us food, take care of the kids.

A few weeks later I posted on Facebook about losing Mark, and about our trip, and I ended the post with this quote:

My whole world has been turned upside down. And sometimes I don't know how to breathe in this new reality and every choice seems impossible. But I'm glad we made that choice to be together on an adventure. When you're faced with a choice, just take the damn trip.

That really resonated with people. I got so many messages from people, telling me about trips they had taken with their family, that had meant so much to them. Or how they had been invited on a trip, and were going to say no, but now they were going to say yes. Or how my story had inspired them to go after a dream they'd been pushing to the side.

I started to think about the hardest things that I've been through. Not just losing Mark—but also losing my dad to cancer when I was 24, losing my job three times, losing my home in a house fire in 2010, going through years of fertility treatments to have our kids.

And I thought about the most amazing things I'd created in my life—having those kiddos, building our Dream Home, building up my business...

I started to ask myself, "What is it that I do *different-ly*—not *better*—than other people, to navigate these things with grace and creativity?"

That's when the Take the DAMN Chance Movement started to take shape. Because it was never *just* about a trip. It's about taking the chance on yourself, taking the chance on the dream that you've been pushing to the side.

And, yes, I say the word DAMN a lot, but it does stand for something. It stands for:

D - Decide and Declare
A - Attend Your Own Party
M - Moments not Minutes
N - Now is the Time

I began to create the Do the DAMN Thing Method® and apply it to my own life. And, using that method, I grew Collaborate.Work to over $300K in 18 months...even while grieving the loss of my husband, even in the middle of the pandemic, and especially while being the Mama I wanted to be to my two kiddos. Then I applied the Do the DAMN Thing Method to building the Take the DAMN Chance Movement and grew that to $300K in 24 months. I focused on using the Method in my parenting, my relationships, my health.

And I used it to bring my biggest, boldest dream to life. When Mark passed away we were about 60 days away from starting our next round of IVF, to have our third child. I've always known I wanted to be a Mama of three and losing that dream, at the same instant I lost the love of my life, felt unfathomable. So I used my own Do the DAMN Thing Method to go after that goal and in July of 2021, 20 months after Mark passed away, I welcomed our third child to the world. Our daughter is named Mirastela, because she is my Miraculous Star.

The Do the DAMN Thing Method has changed my life and I know that it can make a huge impact on yours. The Do the DAMN Thing Method is all about getting clarity and getting into action. And it all starts with crafting Your DAMN Manifesto.

What you hold in your hands is the step-by-step guide to crafting your own DAMN Manifesto and bringing your biggest, boldest dreams to life.

D Decide and Declare

A Attend Your Own Party

M Moments not Minutes

N Now is the Time

MOVEMENT OVER MINDSET

B efore we really dive into creating your DAMN Manifesto, there's something I want to be super clear on—your *mindset* doesn't matter. Now I know that seems really backwards and completely opposite from what you've heard lots of other people say. In fact, often books and programs will spend *a lot* of time trying to get your mindset "right."

But what I'm here to tell you is that it does not matter, and *that* is really good news.

What is far more important, far more critical, is movement. Is it easier to get things done when you have positive thoughts? Absolutely. But the reality is that movement will always be more important than mindset.

If you are waiting until you only have positive thoughts, or are never afraid or anxious, or are never

14

uncertain or scared, I will know exactly where to find you one year from today because you will be in this very same spot. The only way to create amazing things in your life is to get into action. You can get into movement no matter what your mindset is.

It is okay if you are scared—I get scared all the time. But I never let it stop me, at least not for long. The most important commitment that you can make, to yourself and to crafting your DAMN Manifesto, is to get into action, no matter how you are feeling.

Are you willing to make that commitment to yourself?

You are going to have times when you are afraid, anxious, scared, overwhelmed, nervous, and you might be tempted to stop, but your commitment is to get into action. Reminder: you do not have to wait until your thoughts or your mindset is right before you can create amazing things. In fact, again, if you wait until you only have positive thoughts, never feel afraid, never worry, you will always stay stuck right in this exact spot.

So your best and biggest commitment to yourself is to take action, even in small doses. That's why we focus on micro-actions.

A micro-action is the smallest possible action that you will *actually* take. No matter what your goal is, which you will get more clarity around when you create your DAMN Manifesto, you will get there by taking micro-actions. In the beginning your micro-actions will be very, very small—they're designed to be. That's why they are called micro-actions. But trust me—as you go along and build more momentum and get more clarity and confidence, your micro-actions will become bigger, they will come faster, and they will take you even further. The most critical piece is that you have to get started. You have to get into action.

I will talk to you a lot about micro-actions. Remember: the definition of a micro-action is the smallest possible action that you will *actually* take. So if you break things down that need to be done and you still find yourself paralyzed, then you need to break it down even smaller. For example, if your big goal is to start a business and you need to build a website; the micro-action is *not* to create the website, it's not to create the first page. The micro-action is not even to write the first headline. The micro-action might be to just go buy the URL.

If your big goal is to get in the best shape of your life, the micro-action is not to do your first workout. It might just be to go for a walk down the street or buy yourself new shoes. It might not be to get your gym membership, it might just be to decide whether you want to work out at a gym or at home.

If your big, bold dream is to be the best parent possible, the micro-action is not to have a great *day* with your kids. The micro-action might just be to spend 60 seconds with your kids, with your phone turned face down.

All of these things may seem so small, but the truth is that you have to do the *first* action before you can do the second. Too often we derail ourselves by making our actions too big at the start. We think that the only way to succeed is to "go big or go home." We jump from not working out at all to six bootcamp-style workouts a week. From not writing our book to demanding of ourselves we write for an hour each day. From just thinking about our side hustle to expecting to make $10K in our first month.

The problem with this intense energy is that it's not sustainable. You will find yourself petering out quickly and then, too often, getting frustrated or angry with yourself and giving up. Saying something like, "I can never follow through on anything."

That's simply not true. Sadly, you set yourself up for failure by overextending yourself too soon. The good news is that we know the solution to this problem! It's to commit to micro-actions and let the momentum build, so you are supporting yourself to increase your effort as you increase your confidence.

In your commitment to movement over mindset, I want you to commit to 15 minutes of micro-actions every single day. Yes, every single day, 15 minutes of micro-actions towards your goal. I understand that you might want to take a day off from working on your big, bold dream, and that's fine. But you can still do 15 minutes of movement towards bringing this to life, towards getting more clarity, towards building excitement and confidence.

You could even create a list of micro-actions that are your "day off" actions. For example, on my day off, I spend at least 15 minutes on micro-actions: meditating, journaling, working on affirmations, getting clearer on my dream, or simply making myself a cup of coffee, shutting the door to my room and spending 15 minutes making a list of micro-actions I could take in the coming week. Any of these simple actions, when done with intention, can be movement towards a big, bold dream (as long as we're not *only* dreaming! Getting our feet moving is still the most important part.) No matter what it is, you can spend 15 minutes towards creating your big bold dream.

I cannot stress this enough: movement is far more important than mindset. So whenever you're feeling stuck, don't try to think your way out of it. Get into action. And if you need more support around this, go check out the next chapter.

THE PAD METHOD™

A s we discussed in the last chapter, and you will hear me say time and time again, movement is always more important than mindset. But, let's be real, you are still always going to have thoughts, feelings, and emotions. So how do you stay in movement and in action, no matter what feelings you are stuck in? You use what I call the PAD Method.

Before we go into that, I want to explain a little bit about how our thoughts and emotions work. I am trained in what's called the Three Principles, which are Thought, Mind and Consciousness.

This is a very brief overview of The Three Principles; if you'd like to go deeper into this, I highly recommend you check out the work of Sydney Banks.

The idea of **Mind** is that we all have the *ability* to think, we all have the ability to create our experience of life. I think of Mind as the canvas we paint our experiences on.

Thought is *how* we create that experience. We all bring our own filters to every day based on our history and our thoughts. So while many people think that our feelings cause our thoughts, it's actually completely the other way around—our thoughts cause our feelings.

For now, I want to talk more deeply about **Consciousness**. Consciousness relates to our level of awareness and presence in the current moment. We spend a lot of our lives outside of the present moment, up in our thoughts. We're worried about the future or we're thinking about the past. We get caught in a thought spiral that kicks off our anxiety. No matter what it looks like for you, we spend a lot of time up in our thoughts rather than in our body. Our bodies can only ever be in the present moment. But our thoughts can play tricks on us; our thoughts can be anywhere.

You can see this when you consider the difference between fear and anxiety. Fear is an incredibly useful emotion. It's an indicator that there is something dangerous or threatening in your path. There's a tiger in the room; there's a bus barreling down the street towards us; your house is literally on fire. With fear there is action you can take.

21

Too often we confuse anxiety and fear. We think we are scared of something, but really we are scared of the *thought* of something. We think "what would happen *if* a tiger came into the room?" We worry about what would happen *if* a bus came barreling down the street? What would happen *if* my business failed? What will I do *if* I can never become the parent that I want to be? What will happen *if* this fitness program doesn't work? We're not scared of what's *actually* happening. We're scared of the *thought* of it. We think those things are fear, but they're actually all anxiety.

So how do you tell the difference?

Well, if you are in fear or afraid of something, there is an action to take. And the way that you know whether there is an action to take or whether you are in fear is to get grounded in the present moment. And that's where the PAD Method comes into play.

Remember: our bodies can only ever be in the present moment. When we are grounded in our bodies, we can tell whether we are responding to something in the current moment or up in our thoughts. The first thing we have to do is get grounded back in our body, out of the "what if" and back into the "what is."

This is where the PAD Method starts.

The "P" of the PAD Method is Pause and get Present. You want to pause, get grounded, get present in the moment. The way you do that is to just get back in touch with your body. For me, when I need to do this quickly I just rub my fingers across my palm or rub my hands together. I can rub my legs, rub my hands along my legs. I am reminding myself of where my body is, how my body feels.

You can also do it by noticing what is currently around you. This is a pink chair that I'm sitting in. There are lamps lit. I hear the birds. You're noticing the "what is" not the "what if". The "what if" is your thinking, and your thoughts can play tricks on you. So you pause and get present in the moment. You can also do this just by taking a few deep breaths or doing a meditation. I created a meditation for this specifically and you can get it at bevinfarrand.com/manifesto for free.

The second step, the "A", is to Acknowledge. You're going to name what you are feeling. Now, there is no such thing as a good or bad emotion. It's only when we attach meaning to our emotions that they take on a positive or negative connotation. You're not going to try to change how you're feeling; you're not going to judge how you're feeling. You're just going to simply acknowledge it, notice it, name it. "I'm feeling scared. I'm sad. I'm overwhelmed." No judgment, just naming.

The final step in the PAD Method is to Do Something.

This is where you're going to get into your micro-actions to move towards your goal. You set a timer for 15 minutes and you get into action. It does not matter what your mindset is. It doesn't matter what you're thinking. You are just getting into action.

What happens if you try to do that and you're still feeling paralyzed? Then you're just going to do anything. Get up and take a walk, go take a shower, have a dance party with your kids or your best friend. Do something to change your physical state so that you can get out of your thoughts.

That is the PAD Method:

Pause and get Present
Acknowledge
Do Something

I promise you—I have used everything I am teaching you throughout this book. When I was submitting proposals for speaking gigs, there was a day I specifically used this PAD Method. I felt myself completely overwhelmed and drowning in anxiety, and I was paralyzed. So I **Paused**, I got **Present** in my body, I got grounded in the current moment. I **Acknowledged** how I was feeling—I named it. I said, "I am drowning in anxiety." I said that to myself and I said it to other friends. I wasn't in judgment around it, I just named it. And then I **Did something**. In this scenario, I pushed send. I pushed send to submit my proposal to a booking agent. That was what I *did.* I could have also just started working on my keynote slides...or I could have gone on a walk, or gotten on a call with my speaking coach. The goal of the "D" is just to do *something,* to get into action.

I want you to take this PAD Method into the day with you. If you're feeling any kind of emotion that you are uncomfortable with, use the PAD Method—Pause, Acknowledge, Do. And if you're getting into your 15 minutes of micro-actions and you're finding yourself stuck, use this method—Pause, Acknowledge, Do. Get grounded in the present moment, name how you are feeling, and then do your micro-actions. Remember: you are not trying to change how you are feeling or your thoughts, you're not judging how you're feeling or your thoughts. You're simply acknowledging them, noticing them and naming them. It's simple, it's easy to remember, and I know that it can change the way you take action.

P Pause and Get Present

A Acknowledge

D Do Something

Uncovering Your Yes

A bove all else, I am passionate about supporting people, just like you, in bringing their big, bold, crazy ideas to life. And I say crazy with all the respect in the world, because I think the best ideas are the crazy ideas.

As I've had more and more conversations with people about their big dreams, I heard many times, "I don't know what my big dream is. I feel like I've forgotten how to dream." What became so clear to me is that too often we've forgotten how to dream *like children*. Instead we dream like editors, immediately jumping to all of the reasons why our dreams *aren't* possible.

I do believe we all have big, bold dreams, but we've gotten out of touch with dreaming big, dreaming without limits. We've gotten scared to share what our dreams are, for fear that people will laugh at them or shame us for having these dreams. Or maybe you're a parent, and you've been so busy taking care of your family that you've lost touch with your dream. Or you're the type of person who puts everyone else's needs before your own and feel like there just isn't time for you to go after your own dreams.

Well, you hold in your hands the guidebook to uncovering your own YES. Over the next few sections, we are going to walk through some exercises that will help you uncover what that dream is in your heart, the dream you want more than anything else.

Above all, I don't want you living a life with regrets. Whether your dream is starting a business, building a business, adopting a child, getting healthy, developing deeply passionate, connected relationships...whatever it is, no matter what your dream is, it is valuable, worthy, and worth your time and energy and passion.

I am excited and honored to be on this journey with you and I can't wait to see what you uncover. Have fun with this! Dream without limits, and let's see what you discover.

REMEMBERING HOW TO DREAM

T he first step in uncovering your YES is to dream big. As I mentioned before, most of us have forgotten how to dream like children and instead dream like editors. Well, not today! Today you are going to get back in touch with what it's like to dream like a child. You are going to dream without limits, without restrictions, without judgments. This book is really a judgment free zone. I don't have any judgment about the ideas you have or what you choose as your YES, because it is *yours*. It needs to be personal. It needs to be something that inspires you.

The first step in this process is to do a Dream Big Brain Dump. If you want to access a series of guided meditations that correspond to these exercises, you can go to bevinfarrand.com/manifesto. If you've never done a brain dump before, you are going to write down all of the potential, big, bold, crazy dreams that you could possibly go after. Spend at least 15 minutes writing down (or typing) all the ideas that come to mind.

Think about what it was like to dream when you were a kid. Don't worry about whether or not you know *how* to do something yet. I've created some amazing things in my life because I didn't know what I didn't know. I created a live event in Chicago because I didn't know how much work it would be. I just dove in and figured it out along the way. And when we were kids, that's how we dreamed. We thought, "Well, I would just *like* to do that. I would like to be an astronaut. I want to do this thing." But we didn't know all the parts and pieces that went into it. We weren't worried about that when we were dreaming. We were just pulled towards what might be fun.

Think about your big dreams right now. What would be fun? What would light you up? And maybe they don't seem so big to you. Maybe they're smaller dreams, but they're still the thing that lights you up. Truthfully, we sometimes get too caught up in comparing our dreams to other people's, thinking ours aren't big enough, bold enough, flashy enough. But above all, it just has to be *your* dream. It has to be the thing that *you* want to go after.

First things first, you're just going to dream without limits. Don't edit yourself. Don't judge what you put down on the page. Don't even really think too much about it. If it comes to mind, write it down. Writing it down does not commit you to doing it. So you could write down: write a book, write a movie, open a restaurant, all these things, knowing that you don't want to do 90% of them. You'll get into *picking* your dream in the next step. The first step, Dreaming Big, is just getting you back to a place where you remember what it's like to dream at all.

Set a timer for 15 minutes and just write and write and write. Try to keep your pen moving across the paper or your fingers moving across the keys. One of my first coaches would say, "Write until the water runs clear." Just keep coming up with ideas. Don't worry about how you would do it. Don't worry about the logistics. If it's something that only happens in France and you live in Idaho, don't worry about it. That's not where you are right now. You're not focused on the *how*, you're focused on the *what*. Right now you're just trying to get as many ideas onto the paper as possible.

After 15 minutes, if you still feel like you want to keep going, keep going. If some ideas come to you later—in an hour, overnight, tomorrow morning—add them to the list. At the end of this, you will have a really exciting potential list of dreams that *could be yours*. That's it. This step is all about dreaming big, about remembering what it was like to dream without limits, and get it onto the paper.

Now go get to it!

FOCUSING IN

H ow did it feel to spend some time dreaming without limits, letting your mind wander to anything that seems like it might be exciting and getting it onto your page? If you feel like you want more time to simply marinate in those dreams, don't feel like you have to jump right into this section. In The DAMN Manifesto course, we do each of these steps over the course of five days. You don't have to rush this process!

Once you're ready, you're going to focus in. Why? Because when everything is your top priority, nothing is your top priority. You have to choose...at least for now. You have to pick the idea that you're going to go all in on. You might be thinking, "It's only Step 2! How are we already going to do this?" Well throughout this book, you're going to put your YES through some sanity checks. For now, I want you to pick the idea that most excites you. If you want to do a guided meditation first, go to bevinfarrand.com/manifesto.

As you're narrowing things down you might find yourself thinking, "What if I make the wrong choice?" Let me tell you about the best advice I've ever gotten in my life. I was lucky enough to get it when I was 13 years old and, thirty years later, it's still the best advice I've ever received. I had been offered a full scholarship to a boarding school, and I was not sure whether I should go. It was a college prep high school, highly academic, which meant I could probably go to any college that I wanted. But it meant giving up some of the extracurriculars I had become passionate about, not to mention leaving all my friends behind.

My dad and I went to dinner to hash it out because I couldn't decide what the *right* decision was. I was finally getting into a groove at my current school, where I really enjoyed it. We sat and talked for three hours about what to do. At the end of our dinner, he said to me, "Look, Bevin, you're going to make the best decision you can right now with the information that you have at hand. And if in six months, or six weeks, or even six days, you make a different decision, it's because you have more information at hand and you're making the best decision you can with that information you have."

That has helped me so much when I'm making my decisions, because I know I'm always just doing the best I can with the information that I have at hand. As you narrow your choices, remember you are going to make the best decision you can right now.

In addition, there are two phrases I want you to get comfortable with.

- It seemed like a good idea at the time.

- I'm going to pursue this idea until it no longer makes sense to do so.

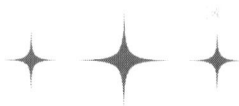

+ ✦ +

It seemed like a good idea at the time

As for the first phrase — it seemed like a good idea at the time — this is one I've used quite often. When I struggle with making a decision and I worry, "What will people think if I don't succeed? What if I fail? What if I'm heading down a path and have to stop? What are people going to think?", I remind myself of this phrase. One of my former coaches said, "Well, just tell them it seemed like a good idea at the time." Of course this is true. In general, we are always trying to make the best decision we can with the information we have at hand. We're not consciously trying to make bad decisions for ourselves. So you can say with confidence that it did, in fact, seem like a good idea at the time. It helps to eliminate some of that stress around the idea of failure.

That is what you are going to do now. You are going to make the best decision you can with the information that you have *right now.*

I'm going to pursue this idea until it no longer makes sense to do so

In 2017, Mark and I pursued the idea of opening a coworking space in our small town. I had gotten wind of impending layoffs and guessed (correctly) that I would be losing my job within the next few months. I loved the idea of creating a space in our community where people could come together. But...we had a 5-month old daughter at home and we knew that it would take a while to build the revenue up. As we looked at spaces and talked to loan officers, I told Mark we would pursue the idea until it no longer made sense to do so.

One night we got into an argument about some of the details. I stayed up late that night, journaling about our idea and going back and forth about the right decision. In the morning I told Mark I thought we should pull the plug. He was surprised but I reminded him that we had agreed to pursue the idea until it no longer made sense to do so. And, since we rarely fought and it was clearly causing us a lot of stress, it no longer made sense to pursue it. Plus, we were about to sign loan papers the next day, and it was going to be a far more expensive decision to end our plans after those documents were signed.

So we decided to give up on that plan, and I'm so glad we did! A few months later, a chain of coworking spaces opened a location around the corner from where we'd been planning. Plus, I got to spend lots of time with my new daughter, working from home at the new job I found and loved.

Just know that you can always pursue your idea until it no longer makes sense to do so. One caveat: it may sound like I'm giving you an easy out here to say, "Oh, I have new information, I'm just making a new decision. It no longer makes sense to go after my YES." That's not how I want you to go into this. I want you to choose an idea that you are willing to go all in on, that you are willing to give your time, energy, focus, maybe some money, and attention towards.

There are going to be days when it gets hard. That's okay, you can do hard things. The reason you are spending the time to discover your YES and crafting your DAMN Manifesto is so that on the days when it does get hard, you have a touchstone to come back to. If you think you might want to completely give up on an idea for a new one, you're going to come back and go through this process again. If you're starting to think that maybe you do want to change directions, you can use my Three Day Rule for Unhappiness

Three Day Rule for Unhappiness

If I am truly unhappy for three days, I know that something is wrong. Not just, "Oh, I kind of don't feel good" or "I'm not sure if I want to keep doing this, it feels hard." I'm talking about the days that I was curled up in the recliner I inherited from my dad (butt-groove and all), bawling my eyes out, because I couldn't imagine working for a company one day more...or in a relationship where every day feels 100% miserable...or every morning you wake up and hate your house. That level of unhappiness. No one should maintain that level of unhappiness for more than three days.

If you are truly unhappy for three days, know that you always have the options to change it, accept it, or remove yourself from the situation. In anything and everything, you can always use this rule. But the three day limit is a good reminder that it's time to check into those options.

But what do they mean?

Let's start with accept it. Accepting is not the same as resignation. Accepting something is not "Okay, there's nothing better out there so I guess this is what I've got." Accepting it is getting to a place where you can accept the circumstances with ease and grace. Sometimes you need to pair this with changing it.

Changing it is iterating, tweaking, making the changes that you need in order to accept it. That might mean you are uncovering more and more about your dream and some of it isn't fitting. For example, maybe the idea you started with is to open up a brick and mortar business. As you start doing your research, you find that there is too much overhead. You don't want to pay rent on a store, you want to spend more time at home, you don't want to be responsible for a store being open certain hours, or having to hire staff. But...you still want to make and sell things. So perhaps you want to start an Etsy store or explore drop shipping. Or you're finding you don't actually want to sell physical products at all!

Maybe you love the idea you've come up with but you don't want to do it by yourself; it's too isolating. So you might want to find somebody to work with.

If you're feeling really unhappy, the first thing to do is check in with yourself about what parts and pieces are making you unhappy? It's rarely the whole. Can you change those parts and pieces?

I once worked for a company where I co-managed a department, and my co-manager and I did not get along. I tried so hard to see things his way, to change the way I communicated, but ultimately I couldn't. It wasn't worth how unhappy I was, hating every time I went into work. I went to the owners and told them I was stepping down. Not quitting, but stepping down from co-managing because I just couldn't make it work.

They asked, "Well, what's the problem?" I explained that I wasn't able to co-manage because I was constantly butting heads with my co-manager. They said, "Let's just split the department." I didn't even think that was a possibility! We split the department—he had his area of expertise; I had mine. All of a sudden the situation had been changed to the point where I could accept it. I was happy with it. Not resigned; happy.

The third option you always have is to remove your-self from the situation. This means you change the dream, or quit the job, or end the relationship. And, yes, we *always* have this option: to remove ourselves from the situation.

It sounds harsh, but I know we never come to these decisions lightly. This is why it is the *Three Day Rule*—three consecutive days of being really unhappy. Because sometimes you may have a really bad day and then realize, "Okay, I was just hungry, confused, and frustrated," and you feel great for three more months. It's not an easy ripcord. It's not, "Oh, you know what? This is harder than I thought. Bevin said that I could just remove myself from the situation."

Remember, this is *your* YES. Not mine. It's yours. You should be excited about it! I want you to be pas-sionate about it, and I want you to bring it to life. Take some time with these exercises. If you want to use a guided meditation to feel confident in your decision to make the best decision for you, right now, you can go to bevinfarrand.com/manifesto to access a free meditation.

Time to Focus In

Get out the list you made in the Dream Big section. You're going to cross out anything that is boring, makes you feel apathetic, makes you feel blah, or that you notice is somebody else's dream. If somebody else really wants you to do it, but it doesn't feel right for you, cross those out!

Next, circle the ones that are most exciting to you. Some might make you feel a little anxious or nervous, maybe even a little afraid. That's okay. That might mean that's the one! That might be the one that challenges you the most, that you're most excited about.

Once you've picked your YES, write it in your journal with as much detail as you want. Remember: you're making the best decision you can with the information that you have at hand. You're going to pursue this idea until it no longer makes sense. Take that pressure off of *needing* to be right. Give yourself 24 hours to sit with your idea. Then it's time to do a good ol' fashioned Gut Check.

GUT CHECK

N ow that you've picked your YES and you've sat with it for 24 hours, how does it feel? Do you feel excited when you think about it? Do you get a little nervous, some butterflies in your stomach?

That's good. That means it's a great dream for you to consider.

If you're feeling bored or apathetic, if you're feeling blah or like you could take it or leave it—it's not your YES. It's not big enough. It's not bold enough. It's not personal enough to be *yours*. Remember: you have to have a YES that even when it gets hard, you are so excited about, it carries you through.

Today we're going to do a solid Gut Check. It's time to really think about if this is the right YES for you. The first question I want to ask, and we've touched on it a little bit already, is this: Is this personal? Is it *your* dream?

A lot of times we have dreams that other people are so excited about us doing, or things that we're good at, so other people think that's what we should do. But it's not really the thing we want in our heart.

The Anti Pro/Con List

Personally, I think the worst decision-making tool is a pros and cons list because you could have 150 items on the con side...and if on the pro side you're thinking, "But I just really want to do it," then I think *that's* the YES you should go for. So, I'm not here to tell you to make a pros and cons list, but I want you to have a gut check with yourself. Is this the dream you want to follow? It might not make sense to anybody else. But it's what *you* want.

Do you think that when I decided to get pregnant as a solo parent, with my third kid with embryos that were frozen from when my husband passed away, that everybody was like, "That's the best idea I've ever heard!"? No. A lot of people thought it was completely crazy. But I knew in my heart that if I didn't do it, it was going to be the thing that when I was 75, I would regret. For me, the decision-making was easy. The execution took work, but the decision was so easy. It was the thing I knew I would always do.

So, that's your first gut check. I want you to take a look at the YES you picked, and I want you to just sit with it and ask yourself, "Is this my dream? The one that if I don't do, I'll feel regret." If you want to spend some time journaling about it, you can. But you can also just sit for a few minutes and check in with yourself. We can learn a lot in the silence.

Our Available Resources

Now I want you to look at your YES, and I want you to think about the resources it's going to take for you to bring to life. This is just planning; this should not scare you. This should not stop you from doing it, but you want to have a clear picture of what it will take.

There are four kinds of resources for you to consider: time, space, energy, and money.

Time

Look at your YES and consider what kind of time you will need to put into your YES in the next three months. How much time each day or each week do you need to carve out in order to bring your YES to life? You can start small and just say 15 minutes a day, 30 minutes a day, or maybe two hours a week. But I want you to be realistic about what you need to put into your YES.

When we think about bringing anything to life, we can approach time in two different ways. We can say "I have 30 minutes a day that I can dedicate to this, which means it will take about a year to complete it." Or we can say, "I want to create this in 3 months so I need to dedicate 2 hours a day to it." Both ways of approaching time are completely valid and it's up to you what is more important. Do you feel inspired to bring your YES to life in a certain amount of time? Or do you want to choose how much time you can dedicate each day or week?

You can play around with this. The more time you put in each day, the shorter the overall time will be. If you think you want to bring this dream to life in six months, and in order to do that you're going to need to dedicate an hour each day to your YES, how does that feel? If that feels like way too much time each day to start out, ask yourself how it feels to bring this to life in a year. Does it feel better? And, let's be honest, often our big YES is going to take longer than a year, and that's totally okay. But play around with the resource of time to where it feels really good to you.

And don't forget that you can always ramp up your time. Maybe you can easily find 30 minutes a day right now...but as the inspiration builds, you might find yourself *wanting* to put more time into bringing your YES to life.

Space

The next resource to consider is space. There are two kinds of space —there's physical space and then there's mental space.

What kind of space are you going to need to create in order to bring your YES to life? Sometimes that means you're going to need to carve out a physical space, a corner of your home, where you can leave your creative supplies out. Do you need to rent a studio or a store? Can you turn an empty bedroom or garage or shed into a work space? I have a writing corner in my bedroom, as well as my home office. What is the space you need?

We also need mental space to have the capacity to create. What do you need to start saying no to, in order to free up some of your mental space? Maybe you need to create space in your calendar, which means you're going to need to start saying no to other opportunities, like volunteering, extra work shifts, or even socializing with friends, for example.

Remember that right now we're not judging the resources. You're just beginning to consider what it is actually going to take for you to realize your YES. You are going to have to make some changes in order to bring something new to life. You can't just keep things exactly the same and expect different results. If that were possible, you would have already brought your YES to life.

Energy

The third resource to consider is energy. You might also think about this as attention or focus. What kind of energy are you going to need to bring to the table to bring your YES to life? Your YES is not going to happen by accident. You are going to need to put some of your energy, attention, and focus into it. Tony Robbins said, "Where focus goes, energy flows. And where energy flows, whatever you're focusing on grows." The things that will grow and flourish and bloom come from where we're putting our focus.

What kind of energy and focus are you going to need to put into this? It could be creative energy. It could be literal physical energy. Especially if your YES is a health journey or something that changes your body, you are going to need to think about physical energy and how you're going to fuel that. What are you going to need to give yourself? How can you best support yourself and the energy you will need to bring your YES to life?

Money

I've intentionally left money for last. Often when we think about our resources, we immediately think of money. Sometimes it's the only resource we think of or we consider it the most important resource. But the truth is that money is the least important resource because it's a *renewable* resource. We can always make more money. We can't, however, create more time or energy.

What kind of money are you going to need to invest into bringing your dream to life? Now, I don't want you to get scared about the money. As with all the different resources, you aren't judging any of these. And with the resource of money, you don't need to think about *where* the money is going to come from yet. You just want to start thinking about what you might need to invest financially to bring this YES to life.

Often with money we get tunnel vision. We think "the only way that I can make money is {insert thing I've always done}." But the truth is that there are so many different ways you can create money. Money is actually the easiest resource for us to create. Time and energy are harder because those are finite. But money can come from hundreds of different sources, and in a later section we're going to do an exercise around how you could create money for your big YES.

+ ✦ +

Where Do You Have an Abundance?

S pend the time to make a list of all the resources that you might need to bring your YES to life. Now, which resource do you have an abundance of? Do you have more time than space, more time than money right now? So many of my friends and clients, when they first start out, have more time than money to invest. So they do a lot of things themselves at first. They Google how to build a website. If they're selling a physical product, they do the packing and shipping themselves at first. They start working out on their own with workouts they found online.

All of that action builds momentum and then they start hiring people to help. Whether it's an employee, or contractor, or a personal trainer, or personal chef, or extra childcare to give themselves more time to work on their big YES. Not only does it build the momentum and maybe start bringing in some money (if it's a business) or extra energy (if it's a health journey or self-care), but seeing the progress also helps us trust ourselves a bit more that we *can* do this.

These different types of resources will dance with each other. There will be times where you have more space than energy, times when you have more money than time, times when you have more time than space.

Which one do you have an abundance of *right now?* Is there anywhere you're going to need to make *immediate* big shifts and changes to make it work?

✦ ✦ ✦

The Way We Create Money

D id you know that most people would rather talk about *sex* than *money?* We've built money up to be this overwhelming, scary thing that is finite and hard to create. But the truth is that money is just an exchange of value. Money doesn't have any inherent emotions tied to it—it's us that assigns emotion to it. So if we are afraid of, excited by, overwhelmed by, or nervous about money, *we* are the ones that are adding that emotion. Yes, it comes from years and years of stories we've told ourselves (or been told) about money, dating all the way back to our childhood. But the *really good news* is that we can change our thoughts at any instant. And this journaling exercise is going to help with that.

One of my favorite, and one of the most effective, ways to explain my view on money involves chickens and cows. When I think about money, I remind myself that the only reason paper money ever came to exist is that it got too hard to walk chickens over for cows.

Think about it. Before money as we know it existed, if someone had two chickens who laid eggs and they wanted a cow that produced milk, they would carry their chickens over to their neighbor and walk home with a cow. Or maybe they carried eggs over and walked home with milk. Or maybe they slaughtered the chicken and traded it for beef.

There were so many ways to get value out of the chickens and the cows.

But walking the chickens over eventually got tedious. What if, instead, we could create a system that assigned value to each item? Maybe a chicken is worth $25 and a cow is worth $50. I could sell two of my chickens for $50 and buy a cow. But I could also choose to buy just a little bit of beef, instead of an entire cow, for $30 and have $20 left over to make improvements to my farm. Or buy grain from another farmer. Or hire a personal trainer (okay, probably wasn't a lot of that happening back then).

Whenever you find yourself overwhelmed or anxious about money, I want you to remind yourself that it's just trading chickens for cows.

When you journaled about money as a resource to bring your YES to life, what number did you come up with? If you didn't come up with a specific number yet, pick one now. Ideally you will pick one that feels a bit out of reach at this point, although this exercise works for any amount of money.

Write that number at the top of a page, or grab the digital workbook at bevinfarrand.com/manifesto.

Now write down the time frame you are giving your-self to create that money. Set a timer for 15 minutes and write down all of the possible ways that you *could* make that money. You are not committing to any of it, so just write down any idea that comes to mind. And you don't have to make the entire amount one way. Maybe you'll make some of it by selling things around your house. Maybe you'll make some by working an extra job. There are literally hundreds, maybe thou-sands, of ways you *could* make money. At this point only write down the idea, not how long it will take or how much you could make.

Once the timer goes off, get up and stretch. I know that thinking about money can cause anxiety and stress, so do something to shake that off. (You know my favorite thing to do is a good dance party!)

When I first did this exercise, my number was $60,000. Holy #%&$, right?! A *huge* number to me, even today. And, to make it even scarier, I only had two weeks to come up with the money. I was starting an apprenticeship for my coaching and, two weeks before my flight, my funding fell through. I was dev-astated. If I moved the start date back then I would miss my first week of training, which happened to be in London, and I would have to cancel a trip to Italy that I had planned to give myself time and space to write and start my business.

A coaching friend of mine introduced me to this exercise and walked me through it. I no longer have that piece of paper, but I know what I wrote down:

Get coaching clients		
Sell real estate (I had my license at the time)		
Sell my condo		
Get a roommate		
Sell my car		
Borrow from ???		
Loan		

I just wrote and wrote and wrote until the time came up. As the fifteen minutes went on, I had to get more and more creative with my ideas.

Once the time was up, I went back and made a note of approximately how much money I would get from each idea and how long it would take.

Get coaching clients	$20,000	6-12 months
Sell real estate (I had my license at the time)	$20,000	3-6 months
Sell my condo	$30,000-$50,000	3-12 months
Sell my car	$5,000	1 week
Get a roommate	$500/month ($6K)	12 months
Borrow from ???	???	???
Loan	$60,000?	30 days?

Now, I will be completely honest...if I were trying to come up with $60,000 today, I would have done it differently than I did it almost 20 years ago. Back then I ended up draining my savings, borrowing some money, and putting some of it on credit cards. I ended up putting myself in a crazy amount of debt and I do not recommend it. I saw it as investing in myself and my business. However, it caused me a lot of stress and eventually I filed bankruptcy. Did I eventually make the money back from my business? I did. But if I were doing it today, I would move the start date back and take some of the pressure off of myself.

Now look at your list and, one by one, go through and make your best guess about how much each idea could generate, and how long that would take. Do you want to make any adjustments to your timeline at the top of the page?

Once you've done that, circle your favorite ideas, the ones that excite you the most. Which one do you want to start with?

The goal of this journaling exercise is to break the tunnel vision we get into around money. Remember: it's just trading chickens for cows. And there are so many different ways we could create money!

+ ✦ +

What Does This YES Mean to You?

The last exercise in this section is to ask yourself, "What would bringing this YES to life mean to me?"

I have full and complete faith that once you create your DAMN Manifesto, you're going to bring it to life. If you pick a YES that gets you excited and you are passionate about, that you are willing to take action towards and keep going, that you go all in on, you will bring it to life.

And what would that mean for you?

Whatever your dream is—getting healthier, adopting a child, starting a business, writing a book, whatever it is—what would your life look like if you brought that dream to life and were living it every day?

Imagine your life in three months. Your YES is beginning to take shape. You're seeing progress and the momentum is starting to build...

Imagine six months from now. What will you have created? What will life look like?

Imagine one year from today. Will your YES be fully realized? What will be different for you? Will you live in the same place? Work at the same job? What will your body look like? How will you feel?

What about in five years? Imagine your life, knowing that you have committed to making your big, bold dream reality? And knowing that you have the capacity to do it *again and again*, with any dream that is important to you.

I also want you to look at the full picture, which is something most people don't do. I do want you to consider any downsides to bringing your YES to life. It's not that I want you to dwell in the negative or get yourself discouraged. I want you to know, when you choose this YES, that it is the right one for you!

Remember when I shared the story about Mark and I opening up a coworking space? When we thought about the downsides, a considerable one was that I would have to be out of the house a big chunk of time. I couldn't work fully from home, which meant that I would have less time to sneak away and see our daughter, and it would be harder to nurse her on demand unless I took her with me, which brought up another set of challenges.

I've previously considered buying an AirBNB, but after Mark passed away, one of the big downsides was that if something were to break in the middle of the night, I wouldn't be able to leave the house to fix it. I would need to hire someone to be on call, and that could significantly eat into any profits.

We want to consider some of the downsides and weigh if they are worth it to us. When I got laid off (for the third time) and decided to start my business instead of looking for another job, one of the downsides was a lack of a paycheck every two weeks. I would no longer have a 401K contribution and would lose my health insurance (although I could go on Mark's at that time. But even now, having to pay for my own insurance as an entrepreneur is something to consider).

I weighed those downsides and still decided that my YES of starting my business was worth it.

I felt how I could impact the financial outcomes of my business by what I put into it. A steady paycheck didn't feel "stable" to me since I'd lost that "stability" three times, with little to no warning. I get to choose how much I do or do not work, and see my revenue fluctuate based on that.

As you're looking at this, remember to fact check your story. One of my clients once told me that a downside to her being super successful was that she would have to get up on stages and speak in front of thousands of people. I asked her, "Says who? You don't *have to* get up onstage, ever." Her downside wasn't even a true story. It was just a story she was telling herself.

If you do see any downsides that pop up for you, it doesn't mean you give up on your YES. But you will want to tweak it until that downside either goes away or is something you can accept.

What happens if you skip over this part of the exercise? Well, you just might find yourself self-sabotaging, and I don't want that for you.

When I have started on any fitness journey, I often self-sabotaged myself and I didn't know why. When I finally thought about it, I realized that I was scared of what extra attention finally hitting my goal weight would bring. When I was younger I had been put in some scary situations and, in my mind, I had associated that with being skinny. Once I saw that fear in my mind, I started to fact check it. I started to do my own healing work on that belief, so that I could navigate fitness and health goals without that fear and anxiety.

In the next chapter, we're going to get even more clear and detailed about your YES. If you have written all of this out and have the feeling of, "Hmmm, I'm not sure this feels like the right dream for me right now," then you can go back to the Focus In section, and see if there is something else that was on your list that you would be more excited about, that would feel like a better fit at this point. And then work through the Gut Check exercises on that idea.

But I do challenge you to find your YES because I know you have it within you, and I know that you also have it within you to bring it to life!

Red Light: The TRIP Filter

I f you haven't figured it out yet, I love a good acronym! Mostly I love them because they are so much easier for you to remember out in the world. And the TRIP Filter is one that you'll end up using pretty much every day (you're actually already unconsciously using it to make decisions). I'm going to show you how you've been using it and then how to apply it to your YES to confidently move forward with it.

The four questions that make up the word TRIP are ones that you can use any time you're making a decision. They are:

Top Priority - Am I willing to make this my Top Priority?

Resource - Am I willing to Resource it?

Inspiring - Is it Inspiring? Is it something I am moving towards, rather than away from?

Personal - Is it Personal? Is it *my* dream?

Think about the last time you bought a car (if you've never bought a car, hang tight because I'll show you how you're also using this TRIP Filter to buy bananas).

The TRIP Filter in Action: Buying a Car

Most of us don't come home to a car in the driveway with a big red bow on it. (Thanks for the dream, Lexus, but it's actually a terrible idea! How many of those gifts get returned because they were the wrong color or model?!) Instead we have to decide that we want a car and then take action towards it. Here's how the TRIP Filter works in this scenario.

Am I Willing to Make It My Top Priority?

If you want to buy a car, that means you aren't going to buy a boat, or a motorcycle, or a timeshare in Bermuda. When most people go to a car dealership to buy a new car, they don't *accidentally* come home with an RV. You've made the decision to make a car your Top Priority *for now* and, within a certain time frame, you come home with a car. The amount of time it takes is directly proportional to how critical your need for a car is. If your old car died on the side of the road, you need a car immediately. If you had your eye on a shiny red convertible, but it's a "nice to have" and not a "need to have," then you might give yourself more time to dream, shop around, and find exactly the right one before you buy.

The same elements are true for your YES:

- You aren't just going to come home one day and find your YES sitting in your driveway, wrapped up with a bright red bow. You are going to have to make it your Top Priority and take action towards bringing it to life.

- When you get clear on your YES, you are going to make it happen. You aren't going to set out to write a book and accidentally paint a picture.

- You are making your YES your Top Priority *for now*. It doesn't mean that you have to become obsessed with this for the rest of your life. You can change your mind because it's not the right fit, or you can complete your YES and move on to another amazing idea.

- The amount of time it will take to bring your YES to life is directly proportional to how critical it is to you. If you are dying to have this

YES in your life, you will make it happen in a shorter time frame. If it's a "nice to have," then you might give yourself more time to bring it to life.

Am I Willing to Resource It?

We already discussed the different types of resources available to us. These resources are available to us for any and all decisions we make.

When it comes to buying a car, we have to make the same decisions about our resources as we do about our YES. Remember: the four main resources are time, space, energy, and money.

Are you willing to dedicate the time needed to research what kind of car would be best for your current situation? Are you willing to spend the time it takes to go to a dealership or search online for cars that might fit, then go do some test drives? If you're buying a car to restore, are you willing to spend the time it will take to bring it back to its original glory? If you're a new driver, are you willing to spend the time learning how to drive?

Are you willing to create space in your life for a new car? It's not going to fit in your mailbox, so are you willing to make space in your garage or your driveway? If you live in a city, are you willing to find a place to park your car?

Are you willing to commit the energy needed to do the research to pick the right car? It's going to take both time and energy to go find the actual car, test drive it, and make the purchase. Are you going to spend your weekend time and energy doing that?

And, yes, it is most likely going to take some money to buy a new car. Are you willing to dedicate some money to buying a new car? Maybe you're going to trade in an old car — are you willing to take the money from the sale of the old car and dedicate it to a new car? Maybe you need to get creative to create the money to buy a new car? Are you willing to spend the energy it will take to come up with ideas and create the money you need that you will then use to buy the new car?

These are the same elements it will take to resource your YES:

- Are you willing to dedicate the time needed to research your YES? Are you willing to spend the time to learn the skills needed to bring your YES to life? Are you willing to carve out time on the weekends, mornings, and evenings to make your YES a reality?

- Are you willing to create space in your life for your YES? Maybe physical space to make it happen or a change in space when it comes to life? Are you willing to move things around in order for your YES to exist?

- Are you willing to commit energy to bringing your YES to life? Are you willing to take your weekend or free time energy and pour it into your YES? When you get home, exhausted from work, are you willing to rally and find the energy you need to move your YES forward?

- Are you willing to allocate some money to bringing your YES to life? Maybe it's only a little bit of money at first, but are you willing to skip a dinner out and spend that $50 on materials needed to create your YES? Are you willing to sell some things that you no longer need to raise money for your YES? Are you willing to get creative in coming up with different ways to make the money needed to start working on your YES?

Is it Inspiring?

Is your YES something you are moving towards rather than away from? You don't go shopping for a car thinking, "I want anything but a motorcycle." You have gotten clear that you want *a car* and you may even know what kind of car: the color, year, the upgrades you want. As you get more clear on the car you want, the picture becomes clearer in your mind and you may even start seeing that color and model of car more often as you go about your day.

You want your YES to be something you are moving towards as well. Our brains can't actually process a negative, so they are going to focus on the concept, not whether it's something that you want or are trying to avoid (we'll go into this more in Cultivating Inspiration).

You also want to feel excited when you think about your YES. Of course there may be a little bit of anxiety with trying something new, but more than anything you should be moving towards something that lights you up, rather than away from something you are afraid of.

When it comes to your YES:

- Is it written in language that inspires you when

you read it?

- Is it something you are moving towards, something you can create?

- When you think about it, do you light up?

Is It Personal?

When you're buying a car, is it the one you want? Does it fit your lifestyle? Is it something you're going to enjoy driving?

My least favorite car was a Pontiac Vibe that I got talked into by the salesperson, who assured me that a sunroof was just like a convertible (spoiler alert: a sunroof is *nothing like* a convertible!). What can I say—I was young, naïve, and needed a car.

My *favorite car* is the bright red Miata convertible that Mark and I bought the summer before our wedding. Even now, with three kids under seven, I have that convertible and love to drive it whenever I am going out without the kids and don't need a car seat.

Look, I live in Ohio. Six months (or more) out of the year a convertible is a totally crazy idea. But Mark and I were so excited about that car and absolutely loved it. So even though it seemed insane, we went for it.

Just like I shouldn't have let that salesperson talk me into his version of a fun car, you don't want to let anyone else dictate your YES. You might be surprised how often people go after *other people's* dreams. Dreams that maybe your parents had for you or dreams that other people want that they think you should also want. As you are thinking about your YES, is it *your* dream? Is it the thing that, when you turn 85 and look back on your life, you know you would regret not doing? That was why having my third child, Mirastela, was such an easy decision. I knew that if I *didn't do it,* it would be the thing that I regretted.

When you think about your YES:

- Is this really the dream *you* want? Or is it something that someone else wants for you?

- When you think about *not* doing it, do you feel a sense of regret or sadness?

- Is it the thing in your heart that you keep pushing to the side? Is it the thing you want, even if it seems totally crazy to other people?

The TRIP Filter in Action: Bananas

Now you've seen one way the TRIP Filter can be used in making big decisions. But we're unconsciously using it every day. And sometimes it's easier for us to look at what we've *done*, so we can see what we *can do.*

Think about the last time you bought a banana. You were using the TRIP Filter to do that, too.

- Did you make buying a banana your Top Priority *for now?* Yes, you did. Bananas don't just show up on your counter (unless you have a magic banana basket...or someone who does the shopping for you). You decided you wanted a banana and took action to make it happen. You didn't go out for a steak and accidentally wind up with a banana.

- You allocated Resources for a banana. Sure, it may have only been $.27 but you allocated that $.27 for a banana. You took the time to shop for a banana (or add it to your Instacart). You spent your energy shopping for, peeling, and eating a banana. You made space on your counter and in your belly for a banana.

- Was it Inspiring? I mean...it's a banana. How inspiring could it really be? But it was definitely something that you were moving towards rather than away from. You weren't thinking, "I do *not* want to eat a watermelon" over and over again until you ended up eating a banana.

- Was it Personal? If you hate bananas, no one can force you to eat a banana once you're over the age of 8. If you're allergic to them, no one can ever make you eat one. People who hate bananas *really* hate bananas. It's a personal decision if you want to eat a banana.

How the TRIP Filter Got Me Pregnant

I saw the TRIP Filter so clearly when Mark and I were in the middle of our fertility journey. I grew up a theater kid and had auditioned for a part I've always wanted to play (Adelaide in *Guys and Dolls*, in case there's a director reading this...). I got called back for the role and was on the phone with my mom, telling her, "I'm so excited to do the show but we're also about to start a round of IVF. What if opening weekend is the same time that we have to do a retrieval or transfer?"

If you've never done theater before, tech week and opening weekend are incredibly grueling. You're doing the dances over and over and over again while they make sure the lights and music and costumes are all exactly how they should be. It's physically and emotionally exhausting.

If you've never done IVF before, it is also physically and emotionally exhausting. It's also timed out very precisely. You are at the mercy of both your body and the doctor's schedule, so if it's time to do an egg retrieval, you have to do it...or wait at least another month. And if you're on a fertility journey, a month feels like a very long time. Plus, when you do a transfer you are supposed to let your body rest for 24-48 hours to give it the best possible chance of success.

Theater and IVF don't really play well together or create the best opportunity for success. And when you are spending tens of thousands of dollars, and desperately want to get pregnant, you want to give it the best possible chance of success.

"Well," my mom said, "maybe you just need to put off IVF for a few months."

Nope. I knew so clearly with every bit of my body that that was not the answer. My Top Priority was not to star in a community theater production. My Top Priority was starting our family. I asked myself:

- Am I willing to make IVF a Top Priority? Hell yeah!

- Are we willing to resource it with time (yes, a lot of time), space (yes, both now and when a baby is hopefully born), energy (whew, yes; lots of energy for shots and appointments and up and down emotions), and money (yes...yikes, so much money!).

- Is it Inspiring? Is it something we are moving towards rather than away from? Yes, absolutely.

- Is it Personal? 100% yes! I always knew that I wanted to be a mom and even drew pictures of myself pregnant while I was in college.

Starting our family was such a clear YES. I hung up the phone and called the director, thanked him for the opportunity but let him know that I would not be at the callback. And about a year later I gave birth to my first daughter.

Run your YES through this TRIP Filter. You can journal about each question if you want or just spend some time thinking each one through. If you don't answer every question with a resounding, "Hell Yeah!" then rework it until you do.

T Top Priority

R Resource

I Inspiring

P Personal

THE PARKING LOT METHOD

I work with a lot of multi-passionate people who have lots and lots of ideas. Lots of them! And often they are hesitant to pick just one YES. They want to start a business *and* write a book *and* move across the country *and* get their yoga certification *and and and.* They have so many brilliant ideas and they want to go after them all, right away.

Here's the thing—you can have everything you want...just not at the same time. You have been working to pick your Top Priority, *for now.* It doesn't mean that you have to give up on everything else you want, and it doesn't necessarily mean that this is going to be the only thing you ever focus on. But you *must* pick your one YES, the thing you want *more than anything else,* for now. Trust me, this is often just as hard for me as it is for you!

In keeping with the theme of the TRIP Filter, imagine you are going on vacation and trying to drive seventeen different cars. You drive the first one a mile and then run back to get the second one. You're really loving how that one feels so you drive it five miles, then run back to get the third one. That third one runs out of gas right away, so you go to the fourth one. That one won't even start, so you jump back over to the first car and drive that one four miles to where you left the second one.

Do you see how none of this is getting you where you want to go? None of the cars are making it to the final destination, and all you're doing is frustrating yourself and wasting a lot of time running back and forth. You're overwhelmed, annoyed, and exhausted. Instead, you could pick your favorite car—that bright red convertible—and drive it all the way to your destination with the top down, great music, enjoying every minute.

This is why I'm passionate about you picking one thing—your YES—and going all in on it. But I know that other ideas might pop up and they might be bright and shiny and grab your attention. That's why you're going to create a parking lot (I'm really going all in on this TRIP Metaphor, I know!)

So what is a Parking Lot? It's an actual repository where you are going to store those other dreams, the other shiny ideas that pop up. Because where you don't want them is up in your head, taking up mental space, spinning around. When you keep them only in your mind, you end up thinking about them more and more, just so you "don't forget anything." We're going to make sure that you don't forget them by giving each one a Parking Spot so you can come back and get them when you are ready.

You can create your parking lot a few different ways. You can use a page for each idea in your journal, or in the DAMN Manifesto Digital Workbook (which you can grab for free at bevinfarrand.com/manifesto if you haven't already). You could also create a folder in a Google Drive and create a document for each idea, or page for each idea in one document. If you use a project management software like ClickUp or Trello, you could create one card for each idea. Whatever you choose, just make it something you can easily access, either on your phone, computer, or a journal you keep with you often, and where you can continue to add ideas and details whenever and wherever they come up.

Let's say your YES is to start a web design business. You've run it through the TRIP Filter and decided that you are ready to go all in on building it. Then a few weeks go by and you think, "What if I started a yoga business? That could be fun. Or maybe I could be a travel writer? Or maybe start an Amazon store?" All of these ideas that keep popping up go into your parking lot. For each idea, get a fresh piece of paper or document or project card and write your idea at the top. You're not going to ignore these ideas and hope they go away and you're also not going to keep them spinning in your mind, taking up brain power. You give each one its own parking spot.

Now any time additional details pop up for those ideas, add them to your parking lot. Maybe you get excited about a specific type of yoga you could teach. Or that you could combine travel writing and yoga by teaching on different beaches throughout the world. Write it down. Add the details, so they are out of your mind and on a page somewhere, safely parked in your parking lot.

Some of these parking spots are going to rust out—you're never going to think about them again. It was one great idea that popped up after a few drinks with friends, but it was really just a flash in the pan and you have no true interest in pursuing it. I've had lots of those! But some of them are going to keep getting attention, and you're going to add more and more details.

If at some point you think, "I might actually be more interested in this; this might be my YES," then I want you to take that idea and run it through the whole process. Maybe you can skip over the Dreaming Big part, but definitely spend the time doing the Focus In, Gut Check and absolutely run it through the TRIP Filter. If you find that it is a more exciting YES, you can park that web design business in your parking lot, just in case you want to come back for it, and go all in on this new YES.

Maybe you're saying to yourself, "Ugh, I don't want to take the time to go through all the exercises again!" Then this new idea is probably not your YES. It's not big and bold enough to unseat your current YES. Trust me, any idea that is worth going after fully is worth the time it takes to run through these exercises, and the rest of the exercises in the book. If it is something you truly want in your life, it is worth the time to create its own DAMN Manifesto because that is going to help you actually bring it to life!

Go create your parking lot right now, wherever you've decided to create it (and you can grab the digital workbook at bevinfarrand.com/manifesto if you haven't yet). Because I know that you have big, bold dreams, and you are going to have another brilliant idea pop up soon and you want to already have your parking lot ready to go, so you can pop it into its own parking spot and then keep moving towards bringing your YES to life. You're not going to give every single idea that pops up energy in your brain any longer. You're not going to ignore it so that it keeps popping up, trying to get your attention. You'll give it its due, acknowledge it, create a parking spot and then move on. Once you've got that created, let's move on to the next step!

Cultivating Inspiration

N ow that you've been sitting with your YES for a few days, how does it feel? Are you getting excited? Does it seem like it's going to open things up in a way that maybe you've never experienced before?

You're going to feel all the feels—you're going to feel excitement, you're going to feel doubt, you're going to feel joy, you're going to feel fear—all those things and that's okay. There are no bad emotions, and you can hold more than one emotion at a time. So, it's good if you're feeling lots of emotions around it. That means you're on the right track.

Now it's time to get inspired. You're going to add some color and some detail into your YES so your whole body gets excited about it.

One thing I know for sure is that our brains cannot process a negative, so we need to make sure our dreams are written in a way that they are something we are moving towards rather than away from. I always say it's a lot easier to want to live in Italy...than to not want to live in Detroit.

Our unconscious mind processes everything we say as a positive statement. It will only focus on the idea, not whether you want it or not. So if you say, "I don't want to live in Detroit," then your unconscious mind thinks about Detroit.

If I tell you, "Don't think about a purple elephant," the first thing you do is think about the purple elephant...then you try to get your mind not to think about it. If instead we shifted to say, "Think about a bright green giraffe," there's no elephant in your mind.

If you think, "I want to quit smoking, stop thinking about smoking," you're going to think about smoking, making it really hard to quit. If you reframe that to thinking about making healthy choices, then of course smoking doesn't fit in with that.

You want your YES to be written in a way that it is something you're moving towards. That means if you're starting a business, you want to think about a thriving, amazing business that supports and inspires you and your family, as opposed to, "I'll do anything if it means I don't have to stay at this job." If your YES is about growing your family, then you think about your loving, healthy family. If it's moving somewhere, think about what it would be like to live in that place.

Take a look at what your YES is and make sure it's written as something that you are moving towards. You also want to use all your senses when imagining your YES. Today you are going to use two storytelling activities to add color to your YES.

One Year Later

Envision what it will look like a year down the road as you bring your YES to life. Write the story of what it is, of how your life looks, of what you've accomplished. So, whatever today's date is, imagine it is one year later. Write the story, in active tense, of where you are and what you are doing.

For example:

> Here I am sitting in my home office, running my brand new business, looking out the window and seeing the river flowing by, smelling coffee that I just made, and hearing my kiddos playing downstairs...

Here I am in the best shape of my life, I weigh X pounds, I've got muscle definition. I just ran my first marathon...

Here I am having adopted my child and I'm sitting in the hospital, holding him or her, feeling the soft blanket in my lap...

Whatever your YES is, write the story of what it will be like in one year, engaging all of your senses.

Dear Me...

It's time to write a letter to your Future Self. Imagine everything you will have created, congratulate yourself, give yourself some advice, give yourself encouragement.

I did this a few years ago during an event, and I'll share what I wrote on December 11, 2020 to my March 2021 self.

Hey there, can you believe how many people have been impacted by Take The DAMN Chance? It's incredible. And it's not just the people in the Facebook community or who have taken the course. It's the people in their lives that have also been impacted because they are showing up differently and connecting more deeply. The ripple effect of this is truly incredible.

And that baby is growing, isn't she? Can you believe she's going to be here in just about five months? This is a dream you've held for so long to have three kiddos, and you made it happen. You did that. And if you can do that, is there anything you can't do? Nope. You can do it all.

I see you. You might still be comparing yourself to those others, but remember: they were in business a long time before they hired you. And you did amazing things for them. Now you get to do those amazing things for yourself. But you are still learning and that's okay. In fact, it's great because everything you need for business is a skill, not a talent. You can learn it, and you are one smart cookie. So, you can definitely learn it.

I know it feels scary to give up one-on-one clients. You might be down to just one now. Wow, that must feel amazing. You must have so much more free time to focus on the impact you make through the Take The DAMN Chance.

Bevin, you are a force. You were meant to make a huge impact in the world. And I'm so glad that you are no longer playing small. I'm glad that you are using your voice and sharing your passion and Doing the DAMN Thing. I'm proud of you, and you should be proud too.

And Guinevere and Jonathan and, soon, the littlest Farrand are going to grow up as such strong humans because they have such a powerful, passionate, empowering mama. You got this, you can do hard things and don't you forget it.

You are so loved.

Me

Let me tell you—so much of what I wrote there came true. I did give up all but one of my one-on-one clients by that date. I was clearly pregnant and gave birth to Mirastela a few months later. I was impacting people by Taking The DAMN Chance. I was envisioning into the future what I saw 90 days later. And so much of it came true.

I want that same thing for you. Write a letter to yourself in 90 days, sharing all of the amazing things you envision for yourself, that *you* will bring to life.

A Vision of Your YES

It's time to engage your sight even more and create a Vision Board. If you've never made a vision board before, these can be incredibly valuable to remind you of what you are working towards, what you are creating.

There are several different ways you can do this.

Poster Vision Board

If you're the type of person who loves a good craft, then this is the way for you. Gather a bunch of magazines, a big piece of cardboard, some scissors and glue. Set a timer for 30 minutes, put on some music, pour yourself a cup of coffee or a glass of wine. Flip through the magazines, tearing out any picture that speaks to you. Don't overthink this—you don't have to use every image you tear out. Don't try to make it pretty; just rip, rip, rip.

Once your 30 minutes is up, start sorting through the images you've torn out and make a pile of the ones that really excite you, the ones that reflect the life you will be living when you bring your YES to life.

Next, arrange them on the cardboard in whatever way is most pleasing to you. Some people like things to be lined up very cleanly and others want things to be more freeform. This is *your* vision board about *your* YES, so however feels best to you is perfect.

Once you feel really good about your vision board, hang it somewhere that you will see it daily. Every time you see it, take a deep breath and feel how good it will be when you are living that new reality.

Digital Vision Board

Some of us (myself included!) prefer things to be digital rather than a poster. If that's you, you can use a free tool, like Canva, to create a digital vision board (I created a special Do the DAMN Thing Vision Board template that you can access at bevinfarrand.com/manifesto). The process is largely the same—collect images and arrange them on a "board" that you can then display wherever you'd like—but there are some differences.

Rather than first tearing out a bunch of pictures from magazines, you can instead search through Canva's library of stock photos or upload images of your own that reflect your goals. You can arrange and rearrange them just by dragging them around. Canva even has templates you can use as guidance.

Once you've got your vision board how you like it, you can save it as your computer desktop, save it to your phone, or print it out if you want the best of both digital and physical worlds. Plus, with something like Canva, you can easily update your vision board if an image doesn't feel quite right.

You could also create a Pinterest board with images and ideas that inspire you and continue adding to it.

Your vision board doesn't have to be complicated. It can be as simple as one picture that really encapsulates your YES, putting it on the window that you look out the most. I have a friend who does these great vision boards, and she really wanted a beautiful back deck. So she found a picture that inspired her, and she put it on the window overlooking the backyard. Every time she looked out that window, she saw it—and she kept it there until the day they built that deck in her backyard.

The goal of the vision board is to engage your conscious and unconscious mind, to "remember" that you are working towards your YES. Every time you see it, feel what it will be like to be living your YES. Remember the previous exercises where you engaged all five of your senses in imagining your fully realized big, bold, wonderful life.

A Vibrant Vision of Your YES

You now have a detailed, exciting vision of your YES between the story of One Year Later, the letter to yourself in 90 days, and a vision board. Are you feeling it? Are you feeling excited and inspired about what you are about to create? Yes? Good! Now, let's move on to the final step in creating your YES.

YOUR SIX-DIMENSIONAL WHY™

N ow that you've gotten really clear on your YES, it's time to dig into your WHY. And not just any old flimsy little why; you're going to fully flesh out what I call your Six-Dimensional Why. You've probably heard people say things like, "What's your why? Start with why! Do it for your why!" And they're right—it is really important to know *why* you want to do something. But these advice givers rarely go far enough.

You can't hang your big, bold dreams on one *flimsy little why.* When it gets hard—and it's always going to get hard at some point—that one why isn't strong enough to keep you going. Instead, when we talk about bringing your YES to life, you want to look at how it will impact the six most important areas of your life. These areas are Financial, Emotional, Mental, Physical, Social, and Spiritual (sorry, I don't have a super easy to remember acronym for this one...yet!).

When you're making a big change in your life, each of these areas is going to be impacted, whether you consider it or not. So, it's really powerful to clearly see how they will be impacted *before* you make this big life change. Once you have your Six-Dimensional Why fully fleshed out, you'll be ready to craft Your DAMN Manifesto.

Let's dive in!

Your Financial Why

The first piece of your Six-Dimensional Why is financial. For a lot of our big, bold dreams the financial element seems pretty obvious or important. If you want to start a business, maybe part of why you want to is for financial freedom or to make more money. It also could initially impact your finances negatively, if you are going to be without income for a while. As you work through the Six-Dimensional Why, you want to look at both the positive and the negative ways these elements of your life are going to be impacted. It's so important to go into this with open eyes and a clear picture of how things may change. It doesn't mean that you are locked into the negative changes. In fact, understanding how things may change in a negative way just allows you to make the plans and tweaks necessary to handle those.

If your YES is to change careers, the financial implications may be very similar to starting a business—you want to make more money or change the day-to-day structure of your work. But the truth is that almost every single YES is going to impact your financial life. Let's look at a few examples:

- If your YES is to get healthier and more fit, how is it going to impact what you're spending your money on, or how much you're spending? Will you hire a personal trainer? Buy organic food? Stop spending money on clothes that don't fit and you never wear?

- If your YES is to move across country, what will you need to spend money on to make the move? How much might you make from selling your home? What will the cost of living change be like?

- If your YES is to build your dream home, what will the cost of building the home be? How will the location change how much you spend on gas and how much time you'll be in the car commuting?

- If your YES is to expand your family, what are the initial costs and the ongoing costs?

Do you see how each YES will impact your financial life? That's not a reason to be scared or to give up on your YES. Remember: there are so many creative ways to make money! But you have to know what you need so you can create an action plan to get it.

When Mark and I decided that we wanted to build our Dream Home, we went through this exercise. Of course, it was going to cost us more money—our mortgage was going to be more. We would have to move twice, because we sold the home we'd been living in and had to move into an apartment while our new home was completed. We had to rent a storage unit (okay, three storage units) to hold our furniture while we were in the apartment. There were so many seemingly negative ways our financial life was going to be impacted.

But we also knew that we wouldn't have to move ever again, (hopefully!) and moving is always expensive. We would be able to give up those storage units. It would shorten Mark's commute. I would have a home office and not have to work at a coworking space.

And most importantly, it was our Dream Home. We were able to design it with so many details exactly how we wanted it. For us, the positives outweighed the negatives. But even if they hadn't, remember, I am anti pro/con list. So even if *all* of the effects seem negative, if you still really want to do it, I say go for it! Above all, clearly understanding the impending impacts is so important in bringing your YES to life.

Spend 15 minutes brain dumping all the ways that your financial life is going to be impacted. You can either do this in your own journal or download the accompanying digital workbook at bevinfarrand.com /manifesto.

Here are some questions you can ask yourself to get started (and then keep going!):

- How could my income change in the short term?

- How could my income change in the next 12 months?

- How could my income change in the long term?

- What am I spending money on now that I could stop spending on?

- What new things/activities/investments could I need to start spending on?

- What financial habits do I want to change?

- What financial habits would have to change in order to bring my YES to life?

- What could change about how I make money?

- What could change about how I save money?

- What could change about how I invest money?

- What could change about how I use money?

- What could change about how I give money?

- What other priorities could be funded that couldn't be before (kids' college tuition, etc.)?

Once you've done that, let's move on to your Emotional Why.

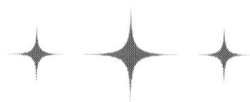

Your Emotional Why

When you bring your YES to life, how is your emotional life going to change? What emotions are you going to start feeling? What emotions are you going to stop feeling?

When Brené Brown started her research for *Atlas of the Heart,* she found that most people could only list three emotions: happy, sad, and angry. If you are having a hard time thinking of other emotions (and you're not alone!), you can download this list of emotions at bevinfarrand.com/manifesto.

As I share examples with you, I don't want you to feel confined by them. When I thought about moving forward with my biggest, boldest, craziest YES—having Mark's and my third child, as a solo parent with two young children already—it made me feel happy, proud, excited, scared, overwhelmed, sad, loving. I thought I would stop feeling frustrated, disappointed, sad.

When I started my business, I thought about how I would feel proud, accomplished, fulfilled, excited, confident. I thought I would stop feeling annoyed, frustrated, disappointed, angry.

No matter what your YES is, think about how you are going to feel when it comes to life, and as you are creating it. And how will you stop feeling? Really dig into the emotions and use that list to help you uncover how you will feel. Go back to your Vision of Your YES and imagine yourself fully living your YES. When you see yourself, one year from now, living your YES, what are you feeling?

When I was making the decision to have Mirastela, I imagined myself holding my new baby, how those first few minutes would feel. What it would feel like to see her take her first steps, how it would feel to see her with her brother and sister. I knew I would feel sadness because Mark wasn't with us. And I also felt all of the joy and pride and overwhelming love and gratitude that she was in my arms. And now that she is two, I have felt all of those things and so much more!

Spend 15 minutes journaling about the emotions. Just keep your hand moving across that page.

Here are some questions you can ask yourself to get started (and then keep going!):

- What emotions do I often feel now that I'd like to stop feeling?

- What emotions do I want to feel more of?

- As I'm bringing my YES to life, what emotions could I feel more of?

- As I'm bringing my YES to life, what emotions could I feel less of?

- Once my YES is fully realized, what emotions could I feel more of?

- Once my YES is fully realized, what emotions could I feel less of?

- When I'm living my big, bold, wonderful life, what emotions do I want to feel when I first wake up in the morning?

- What emotions do I want to feel as I go about my day?

- What emotions do I want to feel before I go to bed at night?

Once you're done, you can move on to the next piece: Mental.

+ ✦ +

Your Mental Why

Just like with the other two elements of your Six-Dimensional Why, it's time to think about how your mental life will change as you bring your YES to life. How are your intellectual life, your thoughts, your overall mental well-being and life going to change?

When I got laid off for the third time and decided to start Collaborate.Work instead of look for another job, I knew that mentally I would feel challenged. I knew I was going to get to learn a lot of new things and solve interesting new problems, which I love to do. I was going to get to decide where to put my focus, what I wanted to learn. This gave me so much mental freedom, which excited me.

I also felt a bit uncertain, which stirred up some emotions (if that's the case for you, you can always add to your Emotional Why). I wondered how I would feel with more mental weight on my shoulders. Again, it was important to get a complete picture, both positive and negative, of the changes that would happen.

When I think about achieving a fitness YES, I think about how I would be able to accomplish anything I truly set my mind to.

Even the goals that might not seem like they would impact us mentally, usually do. Will you be able to free up some mental space because you aren't just thinking about your goals anymore, you're actually bringing them to life? Will you have more mental clarity because you aren't so stressed at a job that you despise? Are you going to feel challenged by writing your book and getting it published?

Set your timer for 15 minutes and journal about all the ways that your mental life is going to change both as you bring your YES to life and once it has happened.

Here are some questions you can ask yourself to get started (and then keep going!):

- What kind of mental challenges do I enjoy?

- When and where do I find myself stuck in thought spirals?

- What will be most mentally challenging about bringing my YES to life?

- What new skills will I get to learn in order to bring my YES to life?

- What am I most excited to learn?

- How do I best learn? How can I incorporate that into my YES?

- What are three ways bringing my YES to life will support my mental well-being?

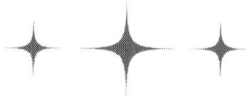

Your Physical Why

You're halfway through your Six-Dimensional Why! Congratulations on all that you have uncovered so far with your YES and the beginning of your Six-Dimensional Why. Please know you don't have to work through this whole process in one sitting. If you need to give yourself a little break, do so! Go for a walk, take a nap, have a cup of coffee or a glass of wine. And you can always go back to each element and add more details as they come to mind.

It's time to dig into how your physical life is going to change. For some YESes, the physical impacts could seem very obvious. But you want to make sure you have a fully fleshed out picture of *how* you are going to be impacted physically, looking at both the positive and negative. If you feel like there are more negatives than positives on one of your lists, it doesn't mean your YES is wrong. You just might want to make some adjustments before really diving in.

When you're thinking about your Physical Why, you want to think about your own body, the physical space around you, the location you live in, your clothes, the food you eat, the products you use—anything and everything that impacts your physical life.

Again, let's look at some examples. When I was thinking about starting my business, instead of going back to work for someone else, I knew that physically I was going to get to work from home. This meant that I was going to be able to spend more time with my kids. I wouldn't be commuting, which saved me at least 2 hours each day, and I would also be able to sneak time between meetings to have dance parties or snuggle time. I would be able to eat lunch with my kids. I could pick them up from school. I also got to easily nurse my youngest kids for the first year, rather than having to pump during the day. All of these things were incredibly important to me and weighed heavily in my decision not to search for a job (and also Mark's and my decision *not* to pursue the coworking space).

As I write this book (another big YES for me), I think about how it will hopefully open doors for me to speak at new events, which will allow me to travel to new places and meet new people.

When I think about a fitness YES, of course it will change my body. But getting healthier will also allow me to more easily run around after my kiddos, wear the clothes I want (and get rid of the extra clothes that clutter up my closet). I'm going to feel better and look the way that I want.

If your YES is to move, across country or to a new home, your physical life is going to be impacted in many ways. If your YES is to expand your family, your body may be impacted immediately, and then your home, as you create space for your new little one.

Think about all of the ways that your YES will impact your physical life and spend 15 minutes brain dumping in your own journal or in the free digital workbook (bevinfarrand.com/manifesto). Remember to write until the water runs clear—just keep your pen moving across the page or your fingers moving across the keys until the timer runs out.

Here are some questions you can ask yourself to get started (and then keep going!):

- Are there any aspects about my body that I currently want to change?

- How will bringing my YES to life impact my body?

- Are there any aspects about my home and where I live that I currently want to change?

- How will bringing my YES to life impact my home and where I live?

- Are there any aspects about my work environment that I want to change?

- How will bringing my YES to life impact my work environment?

- Are there any aspects about my clothes or belongings that I want to change?

- How will bringing my YES to life impact my clothes and belongings?

- Are there any aspects of my activities and how I move in the world that I want to change?

- How will bringing my YES to life impact my activities and how I move in the world?

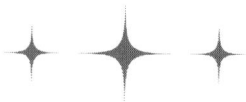

+ ✦ +

Your Social Why

Y ou're on the fifth dimension of the Six-Dimensional Why—you're almost done! I'm so glad that you are sticking with this and really digging into how your life will be impacted when you bring your YES to life. Can you see how often we pick a "why" that isn't fully fleshed out? And when you do that, you're not looking at the entire picture of your life. When this happens, it's so easy to get discouraged as things unexpectedly change.

Trust me, exploring your Six-Dimensional Why this way is going to make Your DAMN Manifesto so much more powerful, so much stronger, and that is going to be a huge catalyst in finally achieving your goals and bringing your YES to life.

This fifth dimension is your Social Why. As you think about bringing your YES to life, how is your social life going to be impacted? This includes your immediate family, your extended family, your social circle of friends and colleagues, your community, and the world. How will the people you interact with be changed by you bringing your YES to life?

When I considered getting pregnant with Mirastela, it was obvious how my immediate family would be impacted—we would be the Farrand Family of Four instead of Three (I promise that my love of alliteration did not play into that decision!). But more deeply than that, how would I have to change as the solo parent of three instead of two? Would I have less time to spend with each of my kiddos, or would I need to interact with them differently? How would it impact how much time I could spend with my other family and friends? Would it impact how often we left the house or how easy it would be to get out and about? How would it impact my extended family to have another little one?

And more than that—with each of my kiddos, I know that I am raising three strong children who will also make an impact on the world. That is another way my decision is impacting society.

As I built my company, and now as I share the Take the DAMN Chance Movement with more and more people, that's making a huge impact on the people close to me, as well as the people who listen to my podcast and read this book. As I speak on stages, I'm impacting the people who listen to me in the room, and also the people in their lives who are impacted as they implement the Do the DAMN Thing Method in their own lives.

With this book, you are being impacted as a reader. But your family, friends, and community are also being impacted by the incredible changes you are making in your life by fully realizing your YES.

Our social life reaches much further than we usually think. Choosing where you work, or whether you want to start your own business, impacts who you get to work with, who you interact with daily as you get coffee from a different location, visit different places, who you get to see in your day-to-day routines. If you start working from home, will you feel more isolated and need to seek out opportunities to interact with people?

If you make a move to a different neighborhood, state, or country, your social life will be impacted in minor and possibly dramatic ways. Maybe you will be closer to people that you know and love, or maybe you will be moving somewhere you know no one (yet).

If your YES is to get healthier and more fit, how will you interact with people differently? Will you go to different events, or go out more or less?

As always, spend 15 minutes doing a brain dump of all the ways your social life will be impacted by bringing your YES to life. It might help to think in circles that expand bigger and bigger (think of a bullseye...or the Target Logo!). Then let's move on to the sixth and final dimension.

Here are some questions you can ask yourself to get started (and then keep going!):

- How could bringing my YES to life impact how I interact with my partner (or future partner)?

- How could my interactions change with my kids (if I have them)?

- How could my interactions with my clients / colleagues / co-workers change?

- How could my interactions with my neighbors change?

- How could my interactions with my extended family change?

- How could my interactions with my close friends change?

- How could my interactions with my community change?

- How could my social media interactions change?

- How could my impact on the world change?

- How could bringing my YES to life impact future generations?

Your Spiritual Why

You did it! You're at the final exercise for the Six-Dimensional Why. By now you're a pro at how to brain dump, so let's dive into your Spiritual Why. Now, to be clear off the bat, this isn't about religion. It doesn't matter what your religion is, or if you don't practice any religion. This is more about your soul's purpose. It might be helpful to think about this as your mission in life. Whatever your YES is, your spiritual life is going to be impacted. Maybe your YES is finally fulfilling a part of your purpose that you've been pushing to the side.

When I made the decision to go all in on the Take the DAMN Chance Movement, that was the case for me. It was a risk to shut down Collaborate.Work. But as I thought about my life going forward, if I never had to talk about another spreadsheet or launch plan ever again, I would be fine. But if I *get to* talk about Mark, my kids, the Take the DAMN Chance Movement and Do the DAMN Thing Method all day, every day...*that* is fulfilling my soul's purpose. I feel it in my core and when I share this, I get chills. That is the impact I want to make on my spiritual life.

When I thought about having Mirastela, I knew that I've always wanted to be a Mama of three kiddos, and I wanted those to be Mark's and my kids. It felt like part of my soul's purpose.

Even when I think about a fitness goal, achieving my YES of being in the best shape of my life impacts my spiritual life because it is aligning my physical body with my mental and emotional being.

There is a reason this is the last dimension in your Six-Dimensional Why—it can feel big and weighty. And to an extent, it is. For many people, your YES will be fulfilling a part of your soul's purpose. It doesn't mean that it has to—I create DAMN Manifestos for just about everything and some of those are less important than others. But when it comes to your biggest YES, it's definitely going to impact your spiritual life.

It's time for your last brain dump for your Six-Dimensional Why. Spend 15 minutes thinking about how your spiritual life—your mission, your soul's purpose—will be impacted by fully committing to your YES and bringing it to life.

Here are some questions you can ask yourself to get started (and then keep going!):

- How does my YES align with my soul's purpose?

- What is most important to me when it comes to leaving my mark on this world?

- Where do I currently feel out of alignment with the essence of who I am?

- How could my YES bring me more into alignment?

- Is there anything about my YES that feels like it might be out of alignment with who I am meant to be?

- When other people tell my story, what are three words I want them to use to describe my impact on the world? How does my YES fit with those words?

- Is there anywhere that I am still playing small with my YES because I am afraid? Am I willing to step more fully into my mission in life through my YES?

CRAFTING YOUR DAMN MANIFESTO

I am so excited that you have your YES and your Six-Dimensional Why fully fleshed out—you should be really proud of yourself. This is such a critical step to bringing a big, bold dream to life and one that so many people skip over. No matter how crazy your dream may seem to other people, you have come so far in finally achieving your goals.

Now that you know what all six dimensions are of the Six-Dimensional Why, let me explain why it's so important to dive into each one. Let's say that your YES is to start a business. More often than not, people will think of the Financial Why and stop there—they want to make more money. Maybe they'll also consider the Physical Why—that they want to be able to work from anywhere. But rarely do they consider all six dimensions. When they're not making enough money, they might give up on their business. Or they're not making enough money and they feel like they can only ever work from their dark basement, so they give up. They think, "This isn't worth it, it will never work, it would be so much easier if I just got a job." But if they had spent the time to fully flesh out their Six-Dimensional Why, it might have looked something like this:

- Financial: I want to make more money and be in control of my income.

- Emotional: I will feel proud of myself and excited that I am creating my own business.

- Mental: I get to use knowledge and skills that I haven't been using in my job.

- Physical: I get to work from anywhere and pick my start and end times each day.

- Social: I get to make a difference in my community and work with some really interesting people.

- Spiritual: This is my soul's purpose, what I was

put on this earth to do.

Now, on the days when they aren't making enough money and are feeling really frustrated, they can rest on how important it is to use knowledge and skills that had been rusting away. Or how much of a difference they are making in their community.

If your YES is to have a family and you have to go through fertility treatments to do that (which I had to do for each of my three kiddos), your Six-Dimensional Why might look something like:

- Financial: This is a big financial investment, but one I am so open to making because I am committed to following this through as far as we can go before exploring other options.

- Emotional: I will feel joy the first time I kiss my new kiddo on the head.

- Mental: I know this is testing my resolve, but I can see how strong I am every day.

- Physical: I am giving my body the absolute best chance to carry a baby and know that if I am unable to do so, it is not because my body is flawed. I will honor and love my body through this entire process.

- Social: I will be the best parent I can be and love my family in whatever shape it takes.

- Spiritual: I am meant to be a parent; it is part of my soul's purpose.

On days when you are emotionally exhausted and physically drained, you can fall back on how this is making you mentally stronger and that being a parent is part of your soul's purpose. This example, in particular, does highlight something to keep in mind. You want to focus on the What ("your YES") and the Why, and release the How. We can't control exactly what the How is going to look like but if we stay committed to our YES and Six-Dimensional Why, then we can be flexible with the How (as well as the When). In the above YES, it's to be a parent and have a family, no matter what shape that takes or how it happens.

If someone's YES is a fitness and health goal, their Six-Dimensional Why might look something like:

- Financial: I will only spend money on clothes that look great, make me feel amazing, and I know I'll wear.

- Emotional: I will feel proud of myself and confident in how I feel and look.

- Mental: I will know that I can accomplish anything I set my mind to.

- Physical: I will look in the mirror each morning and think, "Damn, I look great!" I'll have energy and I'll feel healthy.

- Social: I will feel confident in new social situations and won't be worrying about how I look when I'm out with friends.

- Spiritual: I'll feel my physical body is aligned with the way I feel in my heart and soul.

On the days when the scale isn't moving, they can rest on how proud they feel, and how they will stop filling their closet with clothes that they never wear.

Do you see how powerful it is to have more than just one *flimsy little why?* Do you see that when things get hard—and it's okay that it's always going to get hard—you already know several reasons WHY you are going after this goal, not just one. Again, if you haven't gone through the exercises for all six dimensions, go do that now. You'll have more than just a single sentence for each dimension, and don't feel limited by the examples I've shared. You want to feel so inspired by each Why that you can imagine it with all of your senses.

Now that you have your YES solidified and a clear Six-Dimensional Why, it is time to craft your DAMN Manifesto. This is going to be the touchstone that you come back to over and over as you bring your YES to life.

Your DAMN Manifesto will be your "Yes...in order to...your Why."

When you were in school you probably remember the 5 Ws and an H, right? Who, What, Where, When, Why, and How? Well for now, we are only focusing on the What and the Why. We're going to take your YES and your WHY and make one simple to say, easy to remember sentence.

The first step is to make your YES into a short, simple statement. Remember, you are not focusing on the How at this point. For example, my YES is: "I'm sharing the DAMN Framework with as many people as possible, in as many ways as possible."

Even that might be a little long!

Sample statements might be:

- I am creating a family...

- I am in the best shape of my life...

- I have a business...

- I am writing my book...

If there are specific details that are critical to your YES, include those. For me, it's not just about having a business or speaking on stage—it's critical that I am *sharing the DAMN Framework* in my business and keynotes. My YES would not feel complete without those. I know because I used to have a business executing launch strategy and I used to speak about spreadsheets and marketing, all the time. That didn't light me up!

You've spent the time fleshing out your YES, so this part should be pretty simple. Don't overthink it—you can always tweak it over time. When I first wrote my YES, it was, "I am sharing the DAMN Framework." I added the "with as many people as possible, in as many ways as possible" as it became clear to me that I wanted to write this book, as well as have my digital courses, as well as start my podcast, as well as deliver keynotes....you get the idea.

Now we add in your Six-Dimensional Why. Obviously you have *pages* of reasons why you want to bring your YES to life—that isn't simple to say *or* easy to remember. So you are going to distill that down into one sentence that *triggers* all of those reasons in your mind.

I'll share mine as inspiration: "Create a sustainable, thriving business that both supports *and inspires* my family, and the world."

This encapsulates all six areas of my Six-Dimensional Why which include (but are not limited to):

- Financial: To support my family to live an abundant life—with the activities, travel, etc we want to do—and never have to worry about whether or not I can order an appetizer *and* dessert, or worry about what we buy at the grocery store, or if my kids can do dance *and* gymnastics.

- Emotional: To feel proud of my accomplishments, joy from being onstage, and excited to see how the DAMN Framework changes lives.

- Mental: To challenge myself, learn new skills, and push myself to continue to grow.

- Physical: To get to work from home, so I can spend time with my kids, be in control of my schedule, and travel to new places.

- Social: To change people's lives, meet amazing

people, and inspire my kiddos as they see me as both a business owner *and* a present mom, so they know they can grow up to be anything that they want.

- Spiritual: This is my soul's purpose, it is what I was put on this earth to do.

When I originally wrote my Why it was, "To create a sustainable, thriving business that supports my family." But I realized over time that it was missing a crucial piece—to also *inspire* my family. And then I also realized that it is more than just my family—I want to inspire the world.

Currently, my full DAMN Manifesto is: "I am sharing the DAMN Framework with as many people as possible, in as many ways as possible, in order to create a sustainable, thriving business that both supports and inspires my family and the world."

When I say that, it triggers all of those different reasons why I do what I do. It gets me grounded back in touch with what I am so passionate about. And on the days when the money doesn't feel worth it, I think about how I'm challenging myself and learning new skills. When I'm feeling discouraged, not proud, I remember how I'm setting an example for my kiddos that they can be whatever they want to be when they grow up. And above all, I remember that this is my soul's purpose.

You can always tweak your DAMN Manifesto over time, as more details become clear and you gain more momentum and confidence. Do not let perfect be the enemy of done! For now I want you to craft your DAMN Manifesto to get as close as possible. Spend some time re-reading your Six-Dimensional Why brain dump pages and then take time to craft the second half of your DAMN Manifesto. This doesn't have to happen in five minutes. Write something out, sit with it for a bit and see how it feels.

If you find yourself called to make small changes to your DAMN Manifesto, do it! If you feel like you need to make big changes—or scrap it and start a new one—then simply go back to the start of this book and go through the process again to create a new DAMN Manifesto. If one of your ideas in your Parking Lot starts revving its engine, run it through the TRIP Filter and see if it's a better fit for you to focus on.

Just don't give up on your YES because it gets hard. You can do hard. Just because it's hard, doesn't mean it's wrong. That's why you have your DAMN Manifesto—to stay inspired when things get hard.

Now that you have your DAMN Manifesto, put it out somewhere you can see it every day. You can create an image to print out, use as your computer desktop, or as a phone lock screen by grabbing the Canva templates we created at bevinfarrand.com/manifesto.

Share those designs with me—I would love to see them!

You can send them to:

manifesto@takethedamnchance.com

You can also share on social media with the tag #mydamnmanifesto (and be sure to tag me, too! @bevinfarrand)

THE POWER OF YOUR DAMN MANIFESTO

Your DAMN Manifesto is not meant to just be a pretty graphic that you print out. You spent the time getting clear on your YES and your Six-Dimensional Why because you know that it is time for you to bring that dream to life. Your DAMN Manifesto is the touchstone you will come back to again and again, whenever you are feeling discouraged or frustrated or just need a little extra inspiration.

Whenever I am feeling overwhelmed or like I should give up, I revisit and recommit to my DAMN Manifesto. That might mean that I write it in my journal every morning or before I go to bed. Maybe I'll print out my DAMN Manifesto and tape it in front of my laptop or save it as the lock screen on my phone.

Especially at the beginning of your journey towards bringing your YES to life, lean heavily on your DAMN Manifesto. Say it out loud to yourself. Write it down. Immerse yourself in that DAMN Manifesto as often as you can, to really infuse your entire being with the power of it.

And promise me one thing—do not put it off. I am living proof that we are not promised tomorrow. There is never going to be a perfect Tuesday to get started on your dream. So, if there will never be a perfect day, then why not today?

Now is the Time!

The hardest place to be, when it comes to your YES, is at the beginning because you are standing still. It's always hardest to take the first few steps purely because of inertia. Inertia tells us that an object at rest, tends to stay at rest and an object in motion, tends to stay in motion. Right now you are standing still and it is going to take some extra effort and attention to get your feet moving.

The beautiful thing about this is that once you get your feet moving, momentum will start to take over and keep you in motion. As long as you keep moving, you'll never be at the start standing still again.

Imagine those metal merry-go-rounds that used to be on playgrounds (you know the ones that were usually rusty and creaked and seemed like a deathtrap?). When you ran out for recess and wanted to play on one of those, you and all of your friends would gather around it and everyone would grab a handle. Then all of you would lean forward and push with all of your might to get it started, then keep pushing until it was spinning fast enough and everyone would jump on and it would spin and spin and spin (even thinking about it now kind of makes me want to throw up). If it started to slow down, all you had to do was kick your foot out and give it a little push to keep it going (and pray that you didn't break an ankle!)

That's where you are right now. You've got your hands on the metal bar and you're leaning in to get things started. It's going to take a little extra effort to get it turning but it will get easier. All you have to do is take the first few steps and use your micro-actions.

Remember: a micro-action is the smallest possible action that you will *actually* take. Too often we try to get started with a project and our first actions are way too big! We want to start a business and think that the first thing we need is a website. But that feels so daunting that we never make it.

We want to get healthier and so we sign up for a 90 Day Bootcamp. But that's so overwhelming that we go once or twice and then give up because "we must not be committed enough."

We want to write a book and say, "I need to write for at least an hour every day or it will never happen." (This was me when I started writing this book!)

But we don't need to have this "go big or go home" mentality when it comes to bringing our YES to life! That's how most people burn out quickly and never finish. Instead, with micro-actions, we can break things down and begin building momentum.

When I started the Take the DAMN Chance movement, I didn't start by building a website. I simply bought the URL for $10. Then I wrote the headline. Then I recorded a video. I broke it down into small steps that I would actually take.

If your YES is to get healthier, start by buying a pair of shoes. Selecting a gym. Packing your gym bag. Or even just walking for 10 minutes or doing one bicep curl.

When I tried to write for an hour at a time, I had a hard time finding the time and went for weeks without making any progress. My friend told me that she had written her entire novel in fifteen minute chunks so I gave it a try. And, guess what? You're now reading my book!

When you break things down into micro-actions, if you still find yourself paralyzed then break it down *even smaller.* Over time your micro-actions will get bigger, they will come faster, they will get easier. But for now you just want to get your feet moving with micro-actions you can build on.

Imagine that you are standing at the bottom of a mountain looking at the top. Does it feel impossible to get there? Maybe you decide not to even start because you'll never succeed. Now shift your gaze down and look at the first tree. Could you get to the first tree? I bet you could. Then the next tree...then the next. You could climb an entire mountain just going tree to tree to tree.

Your Micro-Actions

It's time for another Brain Dump (you know I love my Brain Dumps!) Set a timer for 15 minutes and make a list of all the actions you could take to move your YES forward. Don't worry about how long each action might take, or if it's too complicated, or what you might need to make it happen. Just write for 15 minutes, and get as many actions down on the page as you can.

Once the timer goes off, break each of those actions down into micro-actions. The tiniest possible action that you will actually take. Don't be scared to break them down too small—you can always do a series of micro-actions. In fact, everything we do in life is just a series of micro-actions!

Over the next seven days, set aside 15 minutes and work through as many of your micro-actions as you can. Once your timer goes off, you can be done if you want to be. But if you're feeling inspired and want to keep going, do it! When I was writing this book, there were many days when I wrote for 15 minutes and, when the timer went off, I stopped. But there were just as many days when my 15 minutes were up and I kept going. That is the power of momentum—once you're in action you may want to keep going.

Those first few micro-actions are just you grabbing the handle of that merry-go-round and leaning into it. But remember: when you were a kid you didn't wait for the fun to happen before you got started. You knew that once you got on the merry-go-round you would have fun. You took your first few steps with faith in the fun. Do the same with your YES. If you get clear on your YES and get into action, the fun will happen, the results will come. I have faith in you bringing your YES to life and I hope you do, too!

What Next: Bringing Your Damn Manifesto to the World

I hope you've taken the time throughout this book to get really clear on your YES. Get excited about it, really paint the picture in detail of what you are going to create, and what it's going to feel like when you're living it. You've gotten clear on the resources you have at hand to bring it to life—the time, energy, money, focus, attention, space.

Whether you've done this over several days or you've carved out time to work through the entire process in one day, I hope you've spent the time to get in touch with and get excited about your YES. Your dreams are worth this time and focus. Your big, bold, wonderful life is worth this time and focus.

You are worth this time and focus.

Remember: you are making the best decision you can with the information you have at hand. Often people get in their own way, thinking they have to wait until they are sure they are making *the right decision.* But you *are* making the right decision, the best one you can with the information you have at hand.

And now it's time to get into action. It's time for you to Do the DAMN Thing!

With so much love,
Bevin

YOUR DAMN MANIFESTO RESOURCES

I've created additional resources to accompany this book and support you in crafting your own DAMN Manifesto.

Go to bevinfarrand.com/manifesto to enter your name and email address for instant access to these bonuses:

- Your DAMN Manifesto Digital Workbook

- Guided meditations for finding your YES

- Do the DAMN Thing Vision Board Template

- Emotions Guide

- Your DAMN Manifesto Design Templates

FINDING YOUR DAMN PEOPLE

A CHAPTER FROM BEVIN'S 2ND DAMN BOOK

N one of us can create our big, bold dreams in a vacuum. The myth of the solo warrior is just that—a myth. And it's a dangerous one! Because we all need support, and it's rare that we already have enough support in our lives. Once you have your DAMN Manifesto in hand, it's time to start Finding Your DAMN People. My next book is all about that but I don't want you to wait to get started so I've included the first chapter of that book here, so you know how to start building up the support you need!

Decide and Declare

There are two parts to the D in the DAMN Framework: Decide and Declare. If you've crafted your

DAMN Manifesto, much of what you've done so far is Decide. It is the core foundation of the DAMN Manifesto to Decide what it is that you want *more than anything else right now.* What are you so excited about that you are willing to say No to other things in your life? That is your YES, and that is the keystone of your DAMN Manifesto.

But we all know that we can't do everything on our own. And even if we *could,* that doesn't mean that we *should.* At some point you are going to have to start introducing your DAMN Manifesto to the world and that is the Declare piece.

I want to offer a word of caution here. Often people think that "declaring" their idea to the world means shouting it from the social media rooftops. I regularly see people make big, bold declarations on their social media accounts about how this is their million dollar year or this is the year that they lose 50 pounds (these declarations frequently come in January, disguised as "New Year's Resolutions"). Look, I love bold goals. And I love sharing them with the world. But if you share them too soon, you risk derailing yourself and sabotaging the DAMN Manifesto that you are so excited about.

One of my friends and former clients has a t-shirt company called Pebby Forevee. When I interviewed her she shared something that sticks with me, even to this day. She talked about how you can start something, without telling a bunch of people...or anyone at all, and then you can "clap for your own damn self."

You are going to Declare your DAMN Manifesto in a way that builds confidence as you also build support. And you start with picking a team of cheerleaders.

Who Are Your Cheerleaders?

Imagine your DAMN Manifesto as a child. There are some people that you would trust with your newborn baby, right away. And others that you might wait until that baby is a toddler before you have them babysit (and some that you know are going to be that "friend" who takes your 21-year-old to Vegas!)

Right now your DAMN Manifesto is a fledgling, newborn baby dream. You need to be specific and intentional with who you share it with right now. It doesn't mean that you are hiding your DAMN Manifesto or you aren't sure it's the right thing to do. It just means you are going to introduce your DAMN Manifesto to the world slowly, building up a network of support as you do.

Your Cheerleaders are going to be the first 2 to 3 people you share your DAMN Manifesto with, and it's often not the people you think it will be. It's not usually your mom or your siblings, not even always your best friend. Sometimes these people are too close to you and too worried about keeping you safe to be able to simply cheer you on.

Glennon Doyle says, "It's not the cruel criticism from folks who hate us that scares us away from our Knowing; it's the quiet concern of those who love us." Right now you want to pick people who can be excited for you without unconsciously trying to eat away at your dreams.

When I decided to move forward with the IVF that Mark and I had been planning when he passed away, I didn't tell everyone in my life. I picked three close friends and started a text chain with them. I told them their only job was to celebrate with me. They knew that I didn't have Mark with me on this journey but I wanted people to rejoice in the highs and support me through the lows. That meant they could cheer on all the blood tests and ultrasounds and the seven (yes, seven!) pregnancy tests I took. Those went something like "No, Yes, No, No, Yes, Defective, Yes." Yes, I had a defective pregnancy test that *should* have been the tie breaker but instead was a digital test that just flashed a clock over and over, as if to say, "Just wait till you see the doctor."

Not everyone in my life would have been able to stay in the celebration. A few people that I told about my plans early on were so worried that they tried to talk me out of it. So, I stopped talking about it to them. Notice that I didn't stop talking *to them completely.* I just stopped discussing *this particular YES* with them in the early days.

It is okay if some people don't support your DAMN Manifesto right away. But don't confuse Permission with Support.

Permission vs Support

When I understood the distinction between Permission and Support it made a huge difference in my life.

We spend a lot of time unconsciously asking people for permission to go after our dreams. Asking for permission sounds like, "I'm thinking about quitting my job and starting a new business, what do you think?" "I'm thinking about moving to Italy, do you think I should?" "I'm thinking about going after a promotion at work, what are your thoughts?"

The problem with asking for permission is that we are usually asking people we care about, and who care about us. We care about their opinion. And they want to keep us safe, they don't want to see us hurt or upset.

So, they try our dream on for themselves and if they are *at all uncomfortable* they start saying things like, "I don't know...in this economy?" "Who do you know in Italy? You don't even know Italian. Wouldn't you miss everyone here? Maybe just go for a visit." "Do you really feel ready for a promotion? I'd hate to see you try and fail and get upset or rock the boat with your team."

Here's the thing—you are a grown up. You are not a second grader trying to get to the zoo. You don't need *anyone's permission* to go after your big, bold dreams. Instead we ask for support. Support sounds more like this, "I'm going to do this thing and I would love your support. But if you're not comfortable with that, that's okay."

The big difference is that with support, their decision about whether or not to support you is not going to affect *your* decision about whether or not to do it.

It scares so many people in my life that I am an entrepreneur and a speaker and the solo parent of three young children. They are so nervous for me that I don't have a steady paycheck coming in every two weeks. However, since I've been laid off three times in under 10 years, I don't feel like a job is any more stable than running my business (and maybe even less so). These friends and loved ones who are scared for me are not trying to hurt me—they care for me so much that they want to keep me safe. But they are also not the ones who have to live my life and, more importantly, they aren't the ones who would have to live with my regrets.

When I have a new idea for my business, I might ask them for their support. But I am very clear that I don't need their permission. And whether or not they choose to support me, it will not change my decision to move forward.

I know that it can sometimes hurt our feelings, or shake our confidence a little bit, if someone doesn't choose to support us. But it doesn't have to stop you. And it is exactly why you are only picking 2-3 Cheerleaders at this point. Over time, as you get more clarity around the specifics of your DAMN Manifesto and you get more confidence because you're starting to see results, then you'll start to invite more and more people in. But for now, just pick 2-3 people who have the capacity to cheer you on.

How to Ask For Support

We have a hard time asking for, and accepting, the support that we need in our lives. Sometimes we don't want to bother people. Sometimes we feel like everyone around us should know what we need and we shouldn't have to ask for it. But the truth is that asking for the support we want and need does not invalidate the support we get. And since no one is a mindreader, if you don't ask, chances are you won't get it.

The trick is to ask with openness, clarity, and specificity. Whether through an in-person conversation (the best option) or over the phone, email or text, start by saying something along the lines of, "I have this great new idea that I'm very excited about and if you're open to it, I would love your support. I'm starting by sharing this with a very few people that I trust and you are one of those people. I would love to share it with you."

If they're too busy or not excited about your idea, that's okay. It doesn't mean that your DAMN Manifesto isn't a great idea. It only means that there is something in their life that is stopping them from having the capacity to support you.

You also want to be specific about the kind of support you need at this point. You'll notice that when I told my friends that I was thinking about getting pregnant with Mirastela, I was very specific. "I'm starting a text chain. Your job is to cheer me on." It was clear that I wasn't asking for them to go to appointments with me or take on a lot of time or effort. I wanted a text thread dedicated to supporting my big dream.

You also need to give them the space to say no. Recently I had to teach my daughter the difference between a request and a demand, which a lot of us get confused. When we make a request, we allow the person we are asking the space to say no. They may not want to do what we ask, or they may not be able to do what we ask. When it's a request, it is okay for them to say no, without guilt or shame.

If we aren't giving them the space to say no, then it is a demand. Most people don't enjoy demands and can often feel resentful of them. That is not the spirit you want to use when building your team of Cheerleaders. By requesting support, rather than demanding it, you also know they are willingly choosing to support you, which is more exciting anyway!

Pick one person and ask. If they say yes, wonderful! Ask the next person. If they say no, no problem! Ask the next person. Keep asking people until you have 2-3 people who are willing to be your Cheerleaders.

Want more details about Finding Your DAMN People? Sign up bevinfarrand.com/people-book and be in the know!

ACKNOWLEDGMENTS

Well, damn...how in the world do I thank all of the people who Do the DAMN Thing with me?

First and foremost, my family, who consistently shows up for me and loves me fiercely. For my kid-dos—Guinevere, Johnathan, and Mirastela — you are my biggest inspirations, my laughter, my tears, my loves. I hope that our nightly bedtime stories inspire the same passion for reading that inspired my passion to write this book.

For my love, Mark. You were always my biggest cheerleader, my rock, the one who kept me grounded so that I could fly higher. Even without you by my side, you are always in my heart.

My mom and sisters, who have been with me every step of the way, even when you think my ideas are

151

a little bit crazy. My dad, who I miss often and hear in my head frequently. My nieces and nephews, who were my first teachers on how to be a better mom and show my kids how to be a big, loud, silly family. To all of my extended family—when people talk about calm, quiet, low-key family dinners and vacations, I don't quite understand. I feel so lucky to have such an amazing family that supports each other and loves a good board game.

There's no way I could list out all of the friends who have become my family, who have lifted me up when I was curled up on the floor, who have loved my kids and me and Mark with all of their hearts, who inspire me to be the best version of myself. You know who you are and you are always in my heart.

Thank you to my team, both at home and at work. Without you I could not be Doing the DAMN Thing every day. Above all, thank you Juju, Kylie, and Sharon for loving my kids every day so that I can bring this message out to the world. Allison Weedin, my OG VA who I miss daily, and Ashley Chandler for keeping me on track and moving forward. Michelle Rockwell for your guidance and endless support in the speaking world. Dana Malstaff for your help in making the DAMN Framework what it is today. To my early readers and clients who helped shape the DAMN

Framework and gave me insight to where it needed more clarity. Theresa Goodrich, without you this book would still be up in my head and not out in the world.

And perhaps most importantly, you! As you read this book, craft your own DAMN Manifesto, bring your big, bold dreams to life and Do the DAMN Thing, you inspire and amaze me daily. I am here, cheering you on and believing in your big, bold, wonderful life.

ABOUT THE AUTHOR

In 2019, after an unexpected loss just five days after she returned from a whirlwind trip to France with her husband, Bevin Farrand founded the Take the DAMN Chance movement and created the Do the DAMN Thing Method®. Her DAMN framework has inspired thousands to connect with the people that they love, do the "crazy thing" that makes all the difference and, when given a choice, to take the damn chance. Additionally, she is a coach that supports women in achieving their goals, even after going through deeply challenging experiences.